The Farm Family Cookbook

Illinois Farm Bureau®

Marie Kallal, Jerseyville, Jersey County
Joyce Ochs, West Liberty, Jasper County
Shirley Wachtel, Shumway, Effingham County
Savilla Holstine, Milan, Rock Island County

Cookbook Resources LLC, Highland Village, Texas

The Farm Family Cookbook

Illinois Farm Bureau®

FARM BUREAU and FB are registered service marks owned by the
American Farm Bureau Federation.

1st Printing November 2006

ISBN: 9781931294973
Library of Congress Number: 2006936465

Cover Illustrations by Misty Foster

Edited, Designed and Published in the
United States of America
Manufactured in the USA

Cookbook Resources, LLC
541 Doubletree Drive
Highland Village, Texas 75077
Toll free 866-229-2665
www.cookbookresources.com

The Farm Family Cookbook

In true county Farm Bureau grass-roots fashion, four ladies took the lead to help raise funds to expand the *Illinois Agriculture in the Classroom (IAITC)* program by producing and selling this cookbook.

These leaders knew farmers and food are synonymous…as are farm kitchens and great recipes. For decades the wonderful and tasty meals served from Illinois farm kitchens have provided farmers with the energy and nutrition needed to be the most productive in the world. They want to share this bounty through a cookbook of some of the very best recipes from Illinois family farms.

Their vision was to create a cookbook with two goals:
1. To share the sumptuous, nutritious, and bountiful recipes from Illinois farm kitchens.
2. To raise funds to support the *Illinois Agriculture in the Classroom (IAITC)* program.

This cookbook was coordinated by farm ladies who know their way around the kitchen. Their families and friends will attest to the wonderful meals, desserts, and snacks that they have prepared and served.

They have collected and compiled the best from Illinois farm families to share with you. Whether served in their homes, in the field, at a family reunion, or a church bazaar, these recipes have met and passed the test of time, as well as the taste buds of many hungry and hard-working people.

The following Illinois farm leaders are the visionaries, the impetus, the expertise, and the hard work behind the printing of this cookbook:

Marie Kallal, Jerseyville, Jersey County
Joyce Ochs, West Liberty, Jasper County
Shirley Wachtel, Shumway, Effingham County
Savilla Holstine, Milan, Rock Island County

Contents

IAA Foundation Cookbook

Contributors: Tricia Williams **Adams:** Randy Sims **Bond:** Kelli Bassett-DeAngelo, Edith Gaffner **Boone:** Brian Brockmann, John Cleland, Charles Kastning, Ken & Sue Kohley, Brent Mueller, Scot Sell, Connie Spencer **Brown:** Brown County Women's Committee **Bureau:** Alan Dale, Christine Dale, Susan Hildebrand, Mary Kranov, Rheta Schallhorn, Harold & Margery Steele **Calhoun:** Brenda Bizaillion **Carroll:** Reva Doty, Hazel Getz, Mary Holesinger **Champaign:** Elizabeth Rothermel, Loretta Stoerger, Lois Wood **Christian:** Dorothy Bullard **Clark:** Mary Lou Markwell, Rebecca Schiver **Clay:** Chris Hosselton, Eddie Lamb **Clinton:** Jean Brinkmann **Coles:** Becky Metzger **Crawford:** Donna Baker, Karen Dart, Janna Guyer, Holly Inboden, Cheryl Musgrave, Kasey Pruemer, Debbie Siler, Stacey Williams **Cumberland:** Mary Ruth McKinney, Donna Nash, Janet Padrick, Mary St. John, Julie Williamson **DeKalb:** Ruth Aves, Becky Hardt, Sherry Johnson, Scott Newport, Janet Peabody, Miriam Wassmann **DeWitt:** Terry Ferguson, Bob Kuntz, Joan Olson, Brenda Reeser **DuPage:** Marlene Ashby, Ramona Feltes, Gladys Humbracht, Mary Lambert, Penny Meyer, Betty Pauling, Ellen Sietmann, Lyla Striet **Edgar:** Pat Brazelton, Dale & DeAnn Cash, Bill & Jill Higginbotham, Paul & Joy Honnold, Dorene Irish, Doc & Donna Moody, Terry & Debbie Sturgell, Sarah Virgin, Steve & Ellen Webb, Dan & Wanda Winans **Edwards:** Rebecca Greathouse, Chris Heindselman, Elizabeth Lynch, Jamilyn Lynch, Jamilyn Marks **Effingham:** Marilyn Burrow, Gayle Hooks, Jeanette Niebrugge, Michelle Niebrugge, Shirley Wachtel **Fayette:** Stacy Kruenegel **Ford-Iroquois:** Debra Bayston, Terri Jordan, Betty Kelch, Carrie Schumacher, Melanie Warfield, Vivian Ziebart, Beth Zirkle **Greene:** Billye Griswold, Tasha Jordan-Bunting, Becky Kleinmaier **Grundy:** Linda VonQualen **Hamilton:** Jean Delap , Carol Gidcumb, Phyllis Taylor, Phyllis Waibbels, Tonya Wellen **Hancock:** Gayle Pope **Henry:** Jody Curry, Theresa Owens, Ellie Stackhouse, Pat Ufkin, Karen Urick, Lucille Urick **Jackson:** Annette Ehterton, Cheryl Funk, Cheryl Hall, Jackson County Farm Bureau Women's Committee, Dolores McNitt, Lynette Penrod, Jane Tretter **Jasper:** Joyce and Richard Ochs **Jefferson:** Mary Jane Corners, Joyce Dunbar, Nancy Howard, Carmella Kiefer, LaDonna Meyers, LeeAnn Schuette, Joan Williams **Jersey:** Janet Gilworth, Marie Kallal, Wanda Krueger, Wange Krueger, Kim Murray **Kane:** Mary Diehl, Eldon & Sandy Gould, Louise Johnson, Phyllis Kaptain, Janet Medernach, Dorothy Milnamow, Merry Pitstick, Mary Lou White **Kendall:** Sherry Anderson, Jennifer Borneman, Jodi Brummel, Diane Morris, Adele Reedy, Stacy Rehberg, Sarah Stewart **Knox:** Margaret Collis, Rosemary Cowman, Carol Grohmann, Jan Holmes, Lillian King, Erma Reynolds, Frances Sanford, Pat Seaburg, Frances Stegall **LaSalle:** Ruth Jameson, Carmen Nelson **Lee:** Jim & Bernadine Schielein **Livingston:** Brenda Collins, Shari Conard, Rosie Duffy, Teresa L. Grant-Quick, Dennis Haab, Hazel Henkel, Sandra Hoerner, Rolene Jenkins, Jenna Kilgus, Lynn Kimpling **Macon:** Margie Malone **Macoupin:** Kendall & Charlot Cole, Mark Dugger, Jacqui Heyen, Mary Klaus **Madison:** Ruth Becker, Virginia Darr, Helen Eich, Melba Helmkamp, Virginia Herrmann, Tom Jett, Carleen Paul, Frank R. Thomas, Douvain Vieth **Marion:** Evelyn Bartley, Casey Braddock, Marilyn Gerstenecker **Marshall:** The Hausmann Family, The White Family **Mason:** Ron & Lori Armbrust, Mike & Missy Behrends, Brian & Alicia Bell, Randy & Nan Fornoff, Dean & Julie Krause, Kirk & Tammy Martin **Massac:** Dale Faughn, Alma Harris, Orlis Harris, Clint Smith, Debra Travis **McHenry:**, Pat Biggers, Ella Martin, Jean Schiller, Henry Zierer **McLean:**, Gina Medernach, Debbie Meiss, Jayme Thompson **Menard:** Elaine Bachman, Earl & Karon Dugger, Betsy Winkelmann, Jay & Christy Winkelmann **Mercer:**, Susan DeBlock, Sharon Hank, Carol Kiddoo, Janet McCaw, Annette Speer, Margorie Staker, Marjorie Staker, Mary Ann Taylor **Monroe:** Marcella Crook, Darleen Gummersheimer, Adele Hawkins, Jeanette Henry, Carol Howell, Rosalie Ries, Marlene Robert, Eva Schaefer, Karen Schrader, Vicki Taake **Ogle:** Linda Burton, Frances Cappel, Chuck Cawley, Marilyn Hannah, Grandma Ruth Ippen, Edie Wills **Peoria:** Joyce Basehoar, Linda Cramer, Bonnie Ferrell, Jackie Foster, Beth Haney, Marge Hannah, Arlene Heinz, Mrs. Harvey Herrmann, Carol Scherler, Rosene Schielein, Cathy Stahl, Susan Vonk **Piatt:** Dorothy Lange, Rita Vollmer **Pike:** Wanda Borrowman, Tera Hart, Kathy Kendrick **Pulaski-Alexander:** Bonita Hancock, Ginnie Hartman, Flora Helman, Agnes Thurston, Judy Thurston **Randolph:** Richard & Nancy Guebert **Richland:** Elaine Snider **Rock Island:** DeAnne Bloomberg, Julie Bush, Marilyn Bush, Karen DeDecker, Judy Hofer, Savilla & Jim Holstine, Cleone McCulloh, Marty McManus, Tom & Debbie Mueller, Caroline Neumann, Cindy Woodburn **Saline:** Helen DeNeal, Catherine Haney **Sangamon:** Donna Beatty, Dianne Birge, Jodie Brooks, Sue Brooks, Julie Kern-Morrison, Toni Krone, Christina Lauwerens, Mark Reichert, Tammy Yard **Schuyler:** Jean Barron, Haley Kelly, Deana Nell, Sandy Prather in honor of Pat McDaniel, Kelly Westlake **Shelby:** Troy Uphoff **St. Clair:** Nancy Guenther, Elsie Heidenreich, Jane Helms, Joann Hoelscher, Freda Horine, Wanda Mueller, DiAnn Voegele, Laura Whelan, Betty Willmann **Stark:** Bernene Dahl, Lois Dienst, Fran Durbin, Dorothy Schmidt, Tina Squire **Stephenson:** Kathy Brenner, Tina Endress, Sarah Graybill, Nikki Keltner, Ron & Roberta Sluiter **Tazewell:** Mary Farney, Linda Wolters **Union:** Janice Eddleman, Lucille Rich **Vermilion:** Janece Downs **Warren-Henderson:** Mary Ann Allen, David Brint, Tammy Brokaw, Nancy Hall, DeNeene Killey, Paul D. Rickey, Janet Shauman, Maxine Stewart, Amy Thompson **Washington:** RosEllen Greten, Pat Koelling, Edna Newcomb **Wayne:** Mark Bunnage, Delene Reed, David White **White:** Carol Beck, Barbara McArthy **Whiteside:** Paul Kane **Will:** Pat Bleuer, Linda Christiansen, Jane Lagger, Rita Luedtke, Mary Beth Meader, Candy Walz **Williamson:** Jim & LuAnn Anderson, Wanda Robinette, Myrtle Tanner **Woodford:** The Anderson Family, The Gafford Family, The Garber Family, The Goetz Family, The Gray Family, Jan Grebner, Stan Grebner, The Hattan Family, The Kruger Family, Cheryl Pfanz, The Swearingen Family, Beverly Woodward, Mary Zimmerman **Soybean Association:** Carol Meyer

Illinois Farm Bureau®

The Illinois Farm Bureau® is the largest and most influential general farm organization in Illinois. Organized in 1916, its mission is to improve the economic well-being of agriculture and enrich the quality of farm family life.

As a grass-roots organization, with nearly two out every three farmers as members, IFB has been very successful in protecting farmers rights, keeping farmers informed, and making sure farmers have a voice in local, state, and national policy development.

Illinois Agriculture in the Classroom

In 1982 IFB leaders were aware that as the number of farms dwindled, so too did the number of children growing up on farms. This created a concern that as future leaders and policy makers, these children would not understand agriculture and the important role farmers play in providing food, fiber, and now even renewable fuels to them every day. So they created the *Illinois Agriculture in the Classroom (IAITC)* program, which reaches tens of thousands of school children and teachers every year to teach them the importance of agriculture.

It has been so successful that an aggressive growth plan is in place to reach more and more of our future leaders in their classrooms. The plan requires a need to increase funds for programs and activities.

THE DEW'S OFF
LET'S GET STARTED

Appetizers
Dips

Hanky Pankies

1 pound ground chuck
1 pound pork sausage
1 (1 pound) box processed cheese, diced
1 teaspoon Worcestershire sauce
1 teaspoon oregano
½ teaspoon garlic salt
Party rye bread

- Brown meats and drain grease. Add remaining ingredients and ½ teaspoon pepper (except bread). Cook until cheese melts.

- Spread on party rye bread. Place on cookie sheet and bake in 400° for 10 minutes.

Party Sausages

½ pound bacon slices
2 (16 ounce) packages "lil" smokies sausages
Toothpicks
Brown sugar

- Cut bacon slices into 4 equal pieces. Wrap each sausage with 1 small piece bacon. Secure with toothpick. Line 2 large baking sheets with foil and place bacon-wrapped sausages on foil. Sprinkle each with 1 spoonful brown sugar.

- Bake at 425° until bacon cooks (not crispy) and brown sugar melts. Pour smokies and pan drippings into slow cooker. Heat on high for 1 hour. Turn down to low heat and serve.

Porky Ham Roll-Ups

1 (8 ounce) package cream cheese
2 tablespoons mayonnaise or salad dressing
1 teaspoon instant minced onion
1 teaspoon Worcestershire sauce
¼ teaspoon dry mustard
1 (12 ounce) package thinly sliced boiled ham

- Beat together all ingredients except ham and stir until blended. Add ⅛ teaspoon pepper and stir well. Spread 1 tablespoon mixture on each ham slice. Roll up jellyroll fashion, starting at short end. Wrap in plastic wrap and refrigerate. Cut each roll into ¾-inch slices. Yields: 5 dozen.

Confetti Appetizers

1 cup pimento-stuffed olives, chopped
3 green onions with tops, chopped
¾ cup shredded Monterey Jack cheese
¾ cup shredded cheddar cheese
½ teaspoon chili powder
½ cup mayonnaise
8 whole wheat English muffins, split

- Combine all ingredients except English muffins. Cover and chill 2 to 3 hours. Spread cut side of each muffin half with 2 tablespoons cheese mixture.

- Place muffins on cookie sheet and bake 400 for 10 to 15 minutes or until bubbly. Cut each muffin half into 4 wedges and serve warm. Yields: About 5 dozen.

Sweet Onion Kielbasa

1 pound kielbasa sausage
1 small onion, chopped
2 tablespoons butter
1 (12 ounce) can beer
⅓ cup honey
2 tablespoons spicy brown or dijon-style mustard

• Slice sausage into ½-inch slices. Saute onion in butter until transparent.

• In large skillet, slow boil ½ can beer and add sausage. Cook until beer reduces by half and add rest of beer. Add honey, mustard and pepper to taste. Let simmer 5 minutes or until sauce reaches thick honey consistency.

TIP: You can add more onions to finished sauce or add to top as garnish.

The natural yellow color of butter comes mainly from beta-carotene found in the grass cows eat. It takes 21.2 pounds of milk to make one pound of butter.

Ham and Broccoli Crescents

1 (3 ounce) package cream cheese, softened
¼ teaspoon dill weed
1 (8 ounce) can crescent dinner rolls
1 (4 ounce) package thinly sliced ham
1 (10 ounce) package frozen broccoli spears, thawed,
drained

- Preheat oven to 375°. In small bowl, combine cream cheese and dill weed. Set aside. Separate dough into 8 triangles. Cut ham into 8 triangles.

- Spread about 1 teaspoon cream cheese mixture over each dough triangle and top each with ham triangle. Place 1 broccoli spear crosswise on shortest side of each triangle and roll to opposite point. Place rolls points side down on ungreased cookie sheet. Bake for 15 to 18 minutes or until golden brown. Makes 8 servings.

Stuffed Mushrooms

16 - 18 fresh mushrooms
⅓ cup melted butter
1 clove garlic
¼ cup grated mozzarella cheese
¼ cup Italian seasoned breadcrumbs
3 tablespoon grated parmesan cheese

- Remove mushroom stems, chop and fry in butter about 5 minutes. Mix remaining ingredients except caps and add to stems. Stuff caps and bake at 450° for 10 to 15 minutes.

Zucchini Hors d'Oeuvres

1 cup biscuit mix
½ cup finely chopped onion
½ cup grated parmesan cheese
2 tablespoons chopped fresh parsley
½ teaspoon ground oregano
1 clove garlic, minced
½ cup vegetable oil
4 eggs, beaten
3 cups shredded zucchini

• Combine all ingredients with ½ teaspoon salt and ⅛ teaspoon pepper and mix well. Spread evenly in sprayed 9 x 13-inch baking pan. Bake at 350° for 30 to 40 minutes. Let stand 10 minutes before cutting into 1½-inch squares. Makes about 40 squares.

Appetizer Roll-Ups

2 (8 ounce) packages cream cheese, softened
1 (1 ounce) package taco seasoning
1 bunch green onions with tops, thinly sliced
½ (15 ounce) can chopped black olives
4 ounces shredded cheddar cheese
1 (16 ounce) package flour tortillas

• Beat cream cheese until smooth and add seasoning, onions, olives and shredded cheese. Spread thinly on tortillas. Roll each tortilla securely. Place in tightly covered container overnight or 3 to 4 hours until solid. Slice to ½-inch pieces and serve.

Baked Chicken Wings

3 - 4 pounds chicken wings
1 (12 ounce) jar apricot preserves
1 (16 ounce) bottle ranch-style dressing
1 (1 ounce) packet dry onion soup mix

- Lay wings in pan in 1 layer. Mix preserves, dressing, and soup mix and pour over wings. Cover with foil. Bake at 325° for 1 hour. Uncover and bake 20 minutes.

Broccoli-Cheese Nuggets

1 (16 ounce) package frozen chopped broccoli, cooked, drained
1 cup seasoned breadcrumbs
1½ cups shredded cheddar cheese
2 large eggs

- Preheat oven to 275°. In large bowl, combine all ingredients.

- Shape mixture into nuggets and place on sprayed baking sheet 3 inches apart. Bake for 20 to 25 minutes. Turn over halfway through baking time to make extra crispy.

13

Pecan-Cranberry Spread

½ cup cream cheese, softened
¼ cup chopped pecans
¼ cup dried cranberries
⅛ cup orange juice concentrate, thawed

- Beat cream cheese until soft and fluffy with electric mixer on medium speed. Transfer to small bowl, add remaining ingredients and stir. Cover with plastic wrap and chill until flavors blend, at least 30 minutes. Serve cold with crackers. Makes 1 cup.

Sensational Seafood Spread

2 (8 ounce) packages cream cheese, softened
1 (1 ounce) package dry vegetable soup mix
¾ cup cocktail sauce
1 (6 ounce) can crabmeat, drained, flaked
1 (6 ounce) can tiny shrimp, drained
Crackers

- Combine cream cheese and dry soup mix. Spread in serving dish and chill 1 hour. Just before serving, top with chilled cocktail sauce and chilled crabmeat and shrimp. Serve with crackers.

14

Crab Appetizers

2 (8 ounce) packages cream cheese, softened
1 (6 ounce) can crab meat, drained
4 drops Worcestershire sauce
1 tablespoon milk
1 tablespoon mayonnaise
Onion salt
Garlic salt

- Mix all ingredients. Spread on cocktail rye bread slices. Broil at 450° for 2 to 3 minutes.

Holiday Cheese Ball

1 (8 ounce) package shredded mozzarella cheese
1 (8 ounce) package shredded cheddar cheese
2 (8 ounce) packages cream cheese, softened
½ cup chopped ham
1 teaspoon garlic powder
Paprika

- In medium bowl mix all ingredients except paprika and form in ball. Sprinkle paprika on wax paper and roll cheese ball in it until paprika covers completely. Place on plate and serve with crackers.

TIP: You can use chopped nuts instead of paprika if you like.

Sausage-Cheese Balls

½ pound pork sausage
1 (8 ounce) package shredded cheddar cheese
1½ cups biscuit mix
Milk

- Mix pork sausage, cheese and biscuit mix with enough milk to form small balls. (Mixture will be stiff.) Place on baking sheet and bake at 400° for 10 to 15 minutes or until light brown and it cooks through.

TIP: This can be served with hot mustard or favorite sauces. It freezes well and can be used for a brunch.

Pineapple-Cheese Ball

2 (8 ounce) packages cream cheese, softened
2 cups finely chopped pecans, divided
1 (8 ounce) can crushed pineapple, well drained
¼ cup chopped green bell pepper
2 tablespoons chopped onions
1 teaspoon seasoned salt

- Set aside ½ cup chopped pecans, mix all ingredients and chill. Form into ball, roll in remaining pecans and serve with crackers.

Chees-a-Butter

½ cup (1 stick) butter
¾ teaspoon Italian seasoning
⅛ teaspoon garlic powder
½ cup shredded cheddar cheese
1 teaspoon lemon juice

- Beat butter, seasoning, garlic powder and black pepper to taste in medium bowl. Blend in cheese and lemon juice. Form into log shape on wax paper and chill until ready to use. Serve with warm bread.

Caramel Corn

1½ cups large kernel popcorn*
2 cups packed brown sugar
½ cup corn syrup
1 cup (2 sticks) butter
1 teaspoon baking soda
1 teaspoon vanilla

- Pop corn. In heavy saucepan, add brown sugar, corn syrup, butter and 1 tablespoon salt. Bring to rolling boil for 5 minutes and stir constantly.

- Remove from heat and add baking soda and vanilla. Mix well. Pour over corn. Spread corn on several baking sheets. Bake at 200° for 45 minutes and stir often.

TIP: Just so you'll know, 1½ cups popcorn will make 8 quarts popped corn.

17

The Real TV Mix

4 cups Cheerios
4 cups Corn Chex
3 cups Wheat Chex
4 cups Rice Chex
4 cups Crispix
1 (12 ounce) package thin pretzel sticks
3 (2 ounce) cans potato sticks
1 can cashews (unsalted is better)
1 (16 ounce) jar dry roasted, unsalted peanuts
1 (16 ounce) package pecans

- Mix all ingredients in 4 (9 x 13-inch) roasting pans.

2 cups (4 sticks) butter
½ cup bacon drippings
5 teaspoons celery salt
3 teaspoons garlic powder
2 teaspoons onion salt
3 teaspoons hot sauce
3 teaspoons seasoned salt
8 teaspoons Worcestershire sauce
1 teaspoon A-1 sauce

- Melt butter and bacon drippings and stir in all seasonings. Mix thoroughly and pour over cereals; mix well. Bake at 250° for 45 minutes and stir every 15 minutes. Serve when cool.

Brown Sugar Apple Dip

1 (8 ounce) cream cheese, softened
¾ cup packed brown sugar
¼ cup white sugar
2 tablespoons vanilla
1 cup chopped unsalted peanuts
1 (8 ounce) carton whipped topping, optional

• Whip cream cheese, brown sugar, white sugar and vanilla. Fold in peanuts and refrigerate.

TIP: If you want a fluffier dip, fold 2 cups whipped topping into mixture.

Likety Split Lemon Dip

1 (16 ounce) carton sour cream
1 (3 ounce) package instant vanilla pudding mix
¼ cup milk
1 lemon

• Whisk sour cream, pudding mix, milk, 4 teaspoons lemon juice and 1 teaspoon lemon peel in bowl until they blend. Serve with fruit chunks.

Hot Cheesy Salsa Dip

1 pound ground beef, cooked, drained
2 (1 pound) boxes processed cheese, cubed
1 (16 ounce) jar mild or hot salsa

- Place beef in glass baking dish and place cheese on top.
  Pour salsa over cheese. Microwave for 3 minutes covered.
  Stir, continue to microwave and stir at
  3-minute intervals until cheese melts. Serve hot with
  tortilla chips.

TIP: You may use slow cooker to keep warm. This is also good with tomatoes and no-bean chili for a heartier dip.

Cold Salsa Dip

1 (8 ounce) package cream cheese
1 (16 ounce) carton sour cream
1 (16 ounce) jar salsa
1 (8 ounce) package Mexican shredded cheese
Tortilla chips

- Beat together cream cheese and sour cream and spread in
  8 x 8-inch glass dish. Pour salsa ½-inch deep over cheese
  mixture. Top with cheese. Refrigerate about 1 to 2 hours
  before serving.

Fiesta Dip

1 (1 ounce) package fiesta dip mix
1 (16 ounce) carton sour cream
1 (8 ounce) package shredded Mexican 4-cheese blend

• Combine dip mix, sour cream and cheese thoroughly. Delicious with corn chips.

Uncle Bob's Taco Dip

1 (15 ounce) can refried beans
1 (8 ounce) carton sour cream
1 cup real mayonnaise
1 (1 ounce) package taco seasoning
Lettuce
Onions
Shredded cheddar cheese
Tomatoes

• Spread beans on large serving plate. Mix sour cream, mayonnaise and taco seasoning and spread over beans.

• Toss together lettuce, onion, cheese and tomatoes. Cover top of mayonnaise layer. Serve with tortilla chips.

21

Party Dip

1 pound ground beef
2 tablespoons mild chili powder
2 (15 ounce) cans Italian stewed tomatoes with basil, garlic and oregano
1 (8 ounce) package cream cheese, softened
1 (8 ounce) package shredded Mexican 4- cheese blend

- Brown hamburger in large skillet, drain and add chili powder and stewed tomatoes to beef. Simmer 30 minutes.

- Spread cream cheese in a 9 x 13-inch baking pan. Pour beef and tomato mixture over cream cheese. Sprinkle cheese on top. Bake at 350° until cheese melts. Serve with corn chips.

TIP: A hint of lime goes well with this dip.

Reuben Dip

1 (8 ounce) bottle Thousand Island Dressing
2 (2 ounce) packages corned beef, shredded
1 (15 ounce) can sauerkraut, drained
1¾ pounds Swiss cheese, grated

- Combine all ingredients. Place in baking dish and bake at 350° for 25 to 30 minutes. Serve on chips, rye bread or rye crackers.

Corn Dip

1 (8 ounce) carton sour cream
3 - 4 green onions, chopped
2 (11 ounce) cans mexicorn, drained
1 cup shredded cheddar cheese
½ cup mayonnaise
1 teaspoon seasoned salt
½ - 1 teaspoon cayenne pepper

- Mix all ingredients. May add more seasoned salt and cayenne pepper to taste. Keep refrigerated (overnight if possible). Serve with corn chips.

Hot Crab Dip

⅓ - ½ cup milk
½ cup salsa
3 (8 ounce) packages cream cheese
1 (4 ounce) can chopped green chilies
2 (6 ounce) cans crabmeat, drained

- Place all ingredients except crabmeat in bowl and microwave until cream cheese is soft. Stir and add crabmeat. Then put in small slow cooker to keep warm. Serve with crackers or sliced bagels.

Totally Awesome Artichoke Dip

**1 (12 ounce) can artichokes, well drained, finely
  chopped**
1 cup mayonnaise
¼ cup parmesan cheese
½ cup shredded mozzarella cheese

- Mix all ingredients and put in small baking dish. Bake at
  350° for 25 minutes. Serve warm with crackers.

Philly Cheese Dip

1 (8 ounce) package cream cheese, softened
2 tablespoons cream
2 tablespoons salad dressing
1 tablespoon grated onion
⅓ cup ketchup

- Mix all ingredients with ¼ teaspoon salt. Chill overnight
  before serving.

Dill Dip

2 cups mayonnaise
1 (1 pint) carton sour cream
2½ tablespoons dried minced onion
3 tablespoons dill weed
2 teaspoons lemon juice

- Mix all ingredients well. Chill before serving. Serve with
  chips or vegetables.

Bacon-Cheddar Cheese Dip

¾ pound bacon, fried crisp, crumbled
¾ cup finely shredded cheddar cheese
6 green onions, finely chopped
1 cup mayonnaise
3 pecans, finely chopped

- Mix all ingredients and serve with chips.

Round Bread Dip

2 (8 ounce) packages low-fat cream cheese
1 (8 ounce) carton light sour cream
1 (8 ounce) package shredded Swiss cheese
1½ cups light mayonnaise
Green onion, minced to taste
3 (2 ounce) packages corned beef, diced
1 round loaf pumpernickel or sour dough loaf

- Mix all ingredients except corned beef in food processor. Stir in corned beef. Hollow out middle of pumpernickel or sour dough bread loaf. Fill with dip.

- Bake at 325° for 1 hour or until bread is crisp and dip is slightly brown. Serve with torn or cut pieces of bread from hollowed out center. May serve with crackers, but the bread is better!

BLT Dip Delight

2 (8 ounce) packages cream cheese, softened
1 (16 ounce) carton sour cream
2 (3 ounce) packages real bacon bits
2 medium tomatoes, chopped, drained

- Beat together cream cheese and sour cream. Add bacon bits and tomatoes and serve with toast triangles or crackers.

Rye Bread Dip

1 (8 ounce) carton sour cream
1 cup real mayonnaise
1 teaspoon parsley flakes
1 teaspoon onion flakes
1 teaspoon Beau Monde seasoning
1 round loaf German rye bread

- Combine sour cream, mayonnaise, parsley flakes, onion flakes and seasoning. Mix well. Hollow out bread for dip. Tear bread into pieces big enough to dip.

Southwestern Queso

1 pound ground beef
2 (16 ounce) packages cubed processed cheese
1 (8 ounce) package shredded Monterey Jack cheese
1 (10 ounce) can cream of mushroom soup
1 (10 ounce) can tomatoes and green chilies
½ cup milk

- Brown ground beef in skillet, drain and set aside. Place both cheeses, mushroom soup, tomatoes and green chilies and milk; mix well in slow cooker on high heat. Add ground beef and stir frequently. Serve warm with tortilla chips.

Hawaiian Pineapple-Mango Salsa

1 lime, halved
1 (8 ounce) can crushed pineapple with juice
2 mangos
¼ cup diced red bell pepper
¼ cup diced red or purple onion
2 tablespoons cilantro
1 tablespoon rice vinegar
¼ teaspoon ground red pepper flakes

- Squeeze juice from 1 lime half, combine all ingredients in bowl and refrigerate. Adjust lime, cilantro, pepper flakes, etc. as needed. Serve with taco chips.

Sour Cream 'N Bacon Dip Mix In A Jar

This dip mix fills a 1-pint wide-mouth jar.

Mix For Jar:
2 tablespoons dried bacon bits
1 teaspoon beef bouillon granules
1 tablespoon dried minced onion
¼ teaspoon garlic powder

- In small bowl, combine all ingredients, mix well and place one-fifth in small plastic bag. Repeat 4 times to make 4 more bags. Close bags with colorful ribbon and place all bags in jar.

- Place lid and ring on tightly. Use rubber band to secure 1 (7-inch) circle of fabric to lid. Use raffia or ribbon to attach gift tag with following directions.

Directions For Mix In Jar:
1 (1 ounce) packet sour cream and bacon dip mix
1 (8 ounce) carton sour cream

- In medium bowl, combine dip mix with sour cream and stir until mixture blends well. Cover and refrigerate at least 1 hour to allow flavors to blend.

- Serve with vegetables, crackers or chips. Keep refrigerated.

TIP: Plain yogurt, cottage cheese or cream cheese can be substituted for sour cream.

RISE AND SHINE
Brunch

Oatmeal-Buttermilk Pancakes

2 eggs, well beaten
2 cups buttermilk
⅔ cup quick oatmeal
1⅓ cups sifted flour
½ teaspoon baking soda
2 tablespoons sugar

- Combine eggs, buttermilk and oats. Sift flour,
  1 teaspoon salt, baking soda and sugar. Add to egg mixture
  and blend well. Bake on hot griddle. Yields about 20 (4-
  inch) pancakes.

Pancake and Waffle Syrup

½ cup (1 stick) butter
2 cups packed brown sugar
2 tablespoons cornstarch
3 teaspoons vanilla

- Melt butter in saucepan. Add brown sugar and stir well.
  Dissolve cornstarch in 2 cups cold water and pour into
  saucepan. Slowly bring to boiling point and stir to blend.

- Remove from heat and add vanilla. Cover until ready to
  serve. Syrup will keep in refrigerator for several weeks.

*TIP: Should mixture congeal, place over low flame, heat
and thin to desired consistency with hot water. Stir until
smooth.*

Family-Style French Toast

⅔ cup packed brown sugar
½ cup (1 stick) butter, melted
2 teaspoons cinnamon
6 eggs
1¾ cups milk
1 (1 pound) loaf French bread

- Mix brown sugar, butter and cinnamon and pour into 15 x 10 x 1-inch baking pan. Beat eggs, add milk and pour into shallow dish. Cut bread into 1-inch slices, soak in egg mixture for 5 minutes and turn once.

- Put into baking pan and bake at 350° for 25 to 30 minutes or until done. Serve cinnamon side up. Dust with powdered sugar if desired.

Lemon-Poppy Seed Muffins

1 (18 ounce) box lemon cake mix
1 (3 ounce) package instant lemon pudding
4 eggs
½ cup oil
¼ cup poppy seeds

- Mix all ingredients with 1 cup water. Pour into greased muffin tins. Bake at 350° for 20 to 25 minutes.

Stephenson County Dairy Coffee Cake

Topping:
¾ cup sugar
⅓ cup packed brown sugar
1 teaspoon sugar

½ cup (1 stick) butter, softened
1 cup sugar
2 eggs
1 teaspoon vanilla
1 (8 ounce) carton sour cream
2 cups sifted flour
1 teaspoon baking powder
1 teaspoon baking soda

- Preheat oven to 325°. Combine topping ingredients in small bowl and set aside. Cream butter and sugar until they mix well. Beat in eggs and vanilla and add sour cream.

- Add dry ingredients and mix well. Spread half of batter in buttered 9 x 13-inch pan and sprinkle with half of topping. Spoon remaining batter over topping and sprinkle remaining topping on batter. Bake for about 40 minutes, or until cake springs back when lightly touched with finger.

Marvelous Pecan Rolls

½ cup brown sugar
½ cup butter, softened
¼ cup corn syrup
2 (8 ounce) tubes crescent rolls
⅔ cup chopped pecans
¼ cup sugar
1 teaspoon ground cinnamon

- Combine brown sugar, butter and corn syrup. Spread in 2 sprayed 8-inch pans. Open rolls, make 2 rectangles and seal perforations. Combine pecans, sugar and cinnamon and sprinkle over dough. Roll up and seal edge. Cut each into 16 slices. Place in pans.

- Bake at 350° for 15 to 20 minutes or until done. Set for about 1 minute and invert onto serving plates.

Potato Rolls

½ cup (1 stick) butter
1 cup sugar
2 eggs
¼ cup mashed potato flakes
3 (¼ ounce) packages dry yeast
7½ cups flour

- Melt butter in 3 cups water. Add 4 teaspoons salt, sugar, eggs and potato flakes and mix well. While mixture is warm, sprinkle yeast over top and mix. Add flour and knead. Let rise. Shape into dinner rolls and let rise again. Bake at 350 for 10 to 12 minutes.

33

Banana Bread

1¾ cups flour, divided
⅔ cup sugar
2 teaspoons baking powder
½ teaspoon baking soda
1 cup mashed bananas (2 or 3 medium)
⅓ cup butter, melted
2 tablespoons milk
2 eggs

- In large bowl, combine 1 cup flour, sugar, baking powder, baking soda, and ¼ teaspoon salt. Add mashed bananas, butter and milk. Beat with electric mixer on low until mixture blends. Beat on high speed for 2 minutes. Add eggs and remaining flour. Beat until they blend. Pour batter in sprayed 8 x 4 x 2-inch loaf pan. Bake at 350° for 55 to 60 minutes or until toothpick comes out clean. Cool for 10 minutes on wire rack. Makes 1 loaf.

Best Yet Bacon Bread

4 slices bacon, fried, crumbled
1 (3 ounce) package cream cheese
1 teaspoon chopped chives
¼ teaspoon celery seed
Drop of Worcestershire sauce
3 tablespoons mayonnaise
2 tablespoons butter, melted
1 loaf French bread, cut lengthwise

- Mix ingredients and spread on 1 side of loaf. Put top on loaf. Slice through to make 1-inch pieces. Wrap in foil. Bake at 350° for 15 minutes.

Broccoli-Ham Quiche

1 (8 ounce) package refrigerated crescent rolls
4 eggs
½ teaspoon Italian seasoning
1 (9 ounce) package frozen broccoli spears, cut up,
** drained**
1¼ cups cubed ham
1 (4 ounce) jar sliced mushrooms
2 tablespoons chopped green bell pepper
½ cup shredded mozzarella cheese
1 large tomato, peeled, seeded, diced
2 tablespoons parmesan cheese

- Place triangles of crescent rolls in bottom of quiche (or pie) pan. Seal edge and perforations. Press over bottom and up sides of pan. Beat eggs with Italian seasoning and ½ teaspoon salt.

- Place broccoli, ham, mushrooms and green peppers in pastry. Pour egg mixture on top. Put cheese over ingredients in pastry. Bake at 425° for about 15 minutes, turn oven to 350° and bake for about 30 minutes. Quiche is done when knife inserted in center comes out clean. Garnish with chopped tomato and grated parmesan cheese.

Ham and Cheese Quiche

1 cup chopped ham
2 cups grated sharp cheddar cheese
¼ cup minced onion
1 (9-inch) frozen deep-dish piecrust, thawed
2 eggs, beaten
½ cup mayonnaise
½ cup evaporated milk

- Combine ham, cheese and onion and place in piecrust. Combine beaten eggs, mayonnaise and milk. Pour over ham, cheese and onion.

- Bake at 375° for 45 minutes. Quiche is done when knife inserted into center comes out clean.

Farmer's Casserole

3 cups hash brown potatoes
¾ cups shredded cheddar cheese
1 cup diced ham
¼ cup chopped green onions
4 eggs, beaten
3 cups milk

- Arrange hash brown potatoes evenly in sprayed, 2-quart, square baking dish. Sprinkle with cheese, ham and green onions. In mixing bowl, combine eggs, milk, ¼ teaspoon pepper, and ⅛ teaspoon salt. Pour egg mixture over hash brown mixture. Cover and refrigerate overnight. Bake uncovered at 350° for 40 to 45 minutes.

Hearty Breakfast Casserole

12 eggs
½ cup flour
1 teaspoon baking powder
1 (16 ounce) package shredded cheese
2 cups chopped ham
1 (1 pint) carton small curd cottage cheese
¼ cup (½ stick) butter

- Whip eggs and add flour and baking powder. Stir in cheese, ham and cottage cheese. Melt butter in 9 x 13-inch baking dish and pour in casserole mixture.

- Bake at 350° for about 40 minutes or until knife comes out clean. May be made ahead and warmed in microwave.

Brunch Casserole

1 pound bulk pork sausage browned, drained
8 slices white bread, cubed
6 - 8 slices cheddar or American cheese or grated cheese
4 eggs, beaten
2½ cups milk
¾ teaspoon dry mustard

- Place sausage, cubed bread and cheese in layers in sprayed 9 x 13-inch pan. Beat eggs, milk, dry mustard and a little salt and pepper. Pour over bread, cheese and sausage. Refrigerate overnight. Bake at 350° for 45 minutes. Makes 8 servings.

Supreme Sausage Casserole

8 slices bread, cubed
1 pound sausage, browned, drained
1 (8 ounce) package shredded cheddar cheese
¼ cup chopped onion, optional
4 eggs
3 cups milk, divided
1 (10 ounce) can cream of mushroom soup

* Layer bread, sausage, cheddar cheese and onion in sprayed 9 x 13-inch baking dish. Mix eggs and 2½ cups milk and pour over casserole. Mix cream of mushroom soup and ½ cup milk and pour over casserole. Cover with foil and refrigerate overnight. Bake at 300° uncovered for 1 hour.

Hard-Boiled Egg Casserole

½ cup chopped onions
6 tablespoons (¾ stick) butter
6 tablespoons flour
3 cups milk
1 (12 ounce) package grated American cheese
12 eggs, hard-boiled, sliced
2½ cups crushed potato chips
1 (1 pound) package bacon, fried, crumbled

* Saute onions in butter until tender. On medium heat, add flour and mix well. Stir in milk and cook until thick and bubbly. Add cheese and stir until it melts. Layer half of sliced eggs in sprayed baking dish. Pour half sauce over top. Sprinkle half crushed potato chips and half bacon on top. Repeat layers. Bake at 350° for 20 to 30 minutes. Serves 10 to 12.

Scrumptious Scalloped Pineapple

1 (20 ounce) can crushed pineapple with juice
6 slices bread, crumbled
½ cup (1 stick) butter, melted
1 cup sugar
2 eggs, well beaten
2 tablespoons milk

- Combine pineapple and bread and pour into
  9 x 13-inch baking dish. Mix butter, sugar and eggs and
  pour over pineapple. Drizzle milk over top and bake at 350°
  for 40 to 45 minutes.

Spicy Chicken Wings

4 (4 pounds) bags frozen chicken wings
4 cups soy sauce
¼ - 1 cup hot pepper sauce
1 cup vegetable oil
½ cup cornstarch
4 teaspoons ground ginger
2 teaspoons minced garlic

- Place wings on sprayed baking sheets. Bake at 325° for
  50 to 60 minutes. Combine the remaining ingredients
  with 1 cup water in saucepan; bring to a boil and stir
  occasionally. Boil for 2 minutes or until it thickens.
  Transfer wings to large roasting pan and cover with sauce.
  Bake, uncovered, for 60 minutes and stir occasionally.

Pizza Pie

1 loaf frozen bread dough
2 (20 ounce) cans cherry pie filling

Crumb Crust:
⅔ cup sugar
½ cup flour
2 teaspoons cinnamon
¼ cup butter
½ cup chopped nuts

Glaze:
1 cup powdered sugar
1 teaspoon vanilla
1 tablespoon milk

- Roll dough out and place it on greased pizza pan. Form ridge around edge. Pour pie filling on top of dough. Combine all crumb crust ingredients and sprinkle over top.

- Bake at 350° for 35 to 40 minutes. Cool 10 minutes. Combine glaze ingredients and spread over top.

Americans eat the equivalent of 10 acres of pizza (and Mozzarella cheese) every day. The United States produces more than 200 kinds of cheese.

HEART WARMERS

Soups
Salads

Homemade Soup Mix

Keep this dry soup mix ready for instant, homemade soup.
It's a quick fix with a mix.

2 cups nonfat dry milk powder
¾ cup cornstarch
¼ cup instant reduced sodium
Chicken or beef bouillon granules
½ teaspoon dried crushed thyme
½ teaspoon dried crushed basil

- Combine ingredients and store in airtight container.

#1 Cream of Broccoli Soup:
    ⅓ cup Homemade Soup Mix
    ½ cup cooked broccoli florets

- Combine soup mix and 1¼ cup water in saucepan over medium heat and cook until soup begins to thicken. Add broccoli and cook for 15 to 20 minutes or until soup reaches desired consistency.

#2 Cream of Cheese-Broccoli Soup:
    ⅓ cup Homemade Soup Mix
    ½ cup cooked broccoli florets
    ¼ cup reduced-fat shredded cheddar cheese

- Combine soup mix and 1¼ cup water in saucepan over medium heat and cook until soup begins to thicken. Add broccoli and cheese and cook for 15 to 20 minutes or until soup reaches desired consistency.

#3 Cream of Celery Soup:
⅓ cup Homemade Soup Mix
½ cup diced celery

- Combine soup mix and 1¼ cup water in saucepan over medium heat and cook until soup begins to thicken. Saute celery in a little olive oil and add to soup. Cook for 15 to 20 minutes or until soup reaches desired consistency.

#4 Cream of Mushroom Soup:
⅓ cup Homemade Soup Mix
1 cup chopped fresh mushrooms

- Combine soup mix and 1¼ cup water in saucepan over medium heat and cook until soup begins to thicken. Saute mushroom in a little oil and add to soup. Cook for 15 to 20 minutes or until soup reaches desired consistency.

#5 Cream of Chicken Soup:
⅓ cup Homemade Soup Mix
¼ cup cooked, chopped chicken

- Combine soup mix and 1¼ cup water in saucepan over medium heat and cook until soup begins to thicken. Add chicken and cook for 15 to 20 minutes or until soup reaches desired consistency.

Homemakers' Bean Soup

2 pounds dry navy beans
Ham bone
1 large onion, chopped
1 (15 ounce) can tomatoes
1 teaspoon chili powder
1 tablespoon lemon juice

- Wash beans and cover with water in large pan. Add 1 tablespoon salt. Soak overnight. Drain and rinse.

- Place beans in large pan with 2½ quarts water and ham bone. Simmer for 2½ hours. Add more water if necessary. Add chopped onion, tomatoes, chili powder, lemon juice and salt and pepper to taste. Simmer for 1 hour until beans are tender.

Hungry Man's Cheese Soup

2 potatoes, peeled
2 carrots, shredded
2 ribs celery, chopped fine
1 (10 ounce) can cream of chicken soup
1 (10 ounce) can mushroom soup
1 (1 pound) box processed cheese
1 (16 ounce) package frozen broccoli/cauliflower, thawed, finely chopped

- Boil 2 quarts (8 cups) water with potatoes, carrots and celery for 15 to 20 minutes. Add soups and cheese and heat until they melt. Add broccoli and cauliflower. Simmer for 30 minutes or until vegetables are tender.

Uncle Ed's Cheese Soup

5 slices bacon
½ cup grated carrot
½ cup chopped celery
½ cup chopped onion
½ cup chopped green pepper
½ cup all-purpose flour
4 cups chicken broth
3 cups cubed, processed cheese
2 cups milk

- Cook bacon in stockpot until semi-crisp, remove bacon and reserve 1 tablespoon drippings in pot. Set bacon aside. Cook carrot, celery, onion, green pepper until tender, but not brown. Add flour and stir to blend.

- Gradually add chicken broth and stir constantly. Bring to a boil, reduce heat and simmer for 8 minutes until thick. Add cheese and stir until it melts. Stir in milk and ½ teaspoon pepper. Heat over medium heat, but do not boil. Crumble bacon and sprinkle on top of soup.

TIP: A nice addition, but not mandatory, includes
2 tablespoons sherry or ale (beer) and olives.

Did you know that a gallon of milk weighs 8.62 pounds? It takes 10 pounds of milk to make one pound of cheese.

45

Potato Soup

10 - 12 medium potatoes, peeled, diced
1 large white onion, peeled, diced
2 ribs celery, sliced thin
2 - 3 cups milk
1 (10 ounce) can cream of chicken soup
1 (2 ounce) jar real bacon bits

- Cook potatoes, onion, and celery until tender in water. Drain water and add enough milk to cover. Add soup and bacon bits. Heat through to blend flavors.

Cream of Mushroom Soup

1 cup diced onion
3 tablespoons butter
1 pound mushrooms, sliced
1 (14 ounce) can and 1 (10 ounce) can chicken broth
¼ teaspoon garlic salt
2 - 2½ teaspoons cornstarch
1½ cups evaporated milk

- Saute onion in butter in large saucepan. Add mushrooms and cook for 10 minutes. Add chicken broth, garlic salt and ¼ teaspoon pepper. Cover and cook 20 minutes.

- Blend cornstarch with ¼ cup water in separate pan and stir well to remove lumps. Add cornstarch, milk and salt to taste if needed. Heat, but do not boil. Yields: 8 servings.

Cream of Broccoli-Carrot Soup

1 (32 ounce) carton chicken broth
1 (16 ounce) package frozen broccoli
1 small onion, diced
½ pint whipping cream or half-and-half cream
1 small carrot, diced
Garlic

- Combine all ingredients and cook on low until vegetables are tender. Season to taste with salt, pepper and garlic. May add cup sour cream if desired.

Cream of Broccoli Soup

4 teaspoons chicken bouillon granules
2 (10 ounce) packages frozen chopped broccoli
2 tablespoons finely chopped onion
2 (10 ounce) cans cream of chicken soup
2 cups evaporated milk
1 (16 ounce) carton sour cream
1 teaspoon dried parsley flakes

- Combine 2 cups water and bouillon in large saucepan. Add broccoli and onion. Bring to a boil; reduce and heat. Simmer for 10 minutes or until broccoli is tender-crisp. Combine soup, milk, sour cream, parsley and ¼ teaspoon pepper. Add to broccoli mixture. Cook and stir for 3 to 5 minutes or until it heats thoroughly.

Classic Onion Soup

2 cups thinly sliced onions
½ cup (1 stick) butter
¼ cup flour
1 (14 ounce) can chicken broth
2 cups milk
2 cups shredded mozzarella cheese

- In large kettle, saute onions in butter until tender, about 20 minutes. Blend in flour. Gradually add broth and milk. Stir until bubbly.

- Add cheese and stir until it melts. Do not boil. Season with salt and pepper to taste. Yields: About 6 servings.

Orzo-Beef Soup

1½ pounds ground beef
1 onion, chopped
1 teaspoon garlic powder
1 (28 ounce) can chopped tomatoes with juice
½ cup uncooked orzo (barley pasta)
1 (16 ounce) bag frozen mixed vegetables
6 beef bouillon cubes

- Brown beef, add onion and drain. Add remaining ingredients and 6 cups water and 1 teaspoon pepper. Bring to a boil, reduce heat and simmer for 20 minutes, stirring frequently.

Autumn Soup

1½ pounds ground beef
1 onion, chopped
1 cup chopped celery
1½ cups diced potatoes
1½ cups diced carrots
1 bay leaf
1 teaspoon dried basil
1 tablespoon sugar
2 (15 ounce) cans diced tomatoes

- Brown ground beef and onion in skillet and drain. Add all remaining ingredients, except tomatoes and stir in 4 cups water, 2 teaspoons salt and 1 teaspoon pepper. Bring to a boil, cover and simmer for 20 minutes. Add tomatoes and simmer until vegetables are tender. Remove bay leaf.

Mexican Soup

1 garlic clove, minced
2 tablespoons butter
4 boneless, skinless chicken breast halves, cooked, shredded
2 (14 ounce) cans chicken broth
2 (14 ounce) cans chopped, stewed tomatoes
1 (8 ounce) jar mild or hot salsa
½ cup chopped cilantro

- Add minced garlic and butter in slow cooker on HIGH and saute. Combine all ingredients, cover and cook 8 to 10 hours on LOW. Yields: 6 to 8 servings.

Tortilla Soup

1 small onion, chopped
1 cup chopped celery
1 (10 ounce) can tomatoes and green chilies
5 cups chicken broth
1 - 1½ cups cooked, chopped chicken
1 (15 ounce) can pinto beans
½ teaspoon cumin
1 - 2 teaspoons lime juice
2 teaspoons chopped cilantro
2 cups corn chips

- Saute onions and celery in skillet and add tomatoes and green chilies, broth, chicken, beans and cumin. Bring to a boil. Simmer 5 minutes.

- Stir in lime juice and cilantro. Season to taste with salt and pepper. Place corn chips in soup bowls and ladle soup on top.

TIP: There are lots of tortilla soups made many different ways. Choose your favorite and make it yours. If you want it spicier, add a little cayenne pepper. If you want it a little fancier, sprinkle shredded cheese on top.

Terrific Taco Soup

1 pound hamburger
1 medium onion
1 (15 ounce) can corn, drained
2 (15 ounce) cans pinto beans
1 (15 ounce) can tomato sauce
2 (15 ounce) cans diced tomatoes
1 (10 ounce) can mild tomatoes with green chilies
1 (1 ounce) envelope taco seasoning (dry)
1 (1 ounce) package ranch dressing mix

- Brown hamburger in large skillet and drain. Add chopped onion and brown lightly. Add remaining ingredients and simmer. Serve hot.

Slow-Cooker Chili Soup

2 pounds ground beef
1 medium onion
3 (10 ounce) cans tomato soup
½ cup uncooked spaghetti
1 (15 ounces) can red beans
2 teaspoons chili powder
Brown sugar to taste

- Brown ground beef and onion and season with a little salt and pepper. Drain meat mixture on paper towel. In 3½-quart slow cooker, pour in soup, 3 soup cans water, spaghetti, beans and seasoning. Cook on LOW for 6 to 8 hours or on HIGH for 4 hours.

Hearty Hamburger Soup

1 pound lean ground beef
4 beef bouillon cubes
1 (46 ounce) can V8® juice
1 (28 ounce) can diced tomatoes
2 onions, chopped
4 - 5 carrots, sliced
5 - 6 ribs celery, chopped

- Brown ground beef with a little oil in skillet, drain and transfer to large soup pot. Dissolve bouillon cubes in 2 cups hot water and add to soup pot. Mix all remaining ingredients in soup pot and cook until vegetables are tender.

Beef and Barley Soup

1 pound lean ground beef
1 cup chopped onion
1 cup chopped carrots
1 cup chopped celery
2 cloves garlic, minced
1 (32 ounce) carton beef broth
1 (14 ounce) can Italian-style stewed tomatoes
½ cup quick-cooking barley
½ teaspoon dried thyme, crushed

- Brown beef in large skillet, stir in onions, carrots, celery and garlic and cook until vegetables are tender. Drain fat. Stir in broth, tomatoes, barley, ¼ cup water and thyme. Bring to boil and reduce heat. Cover and simmer for 20 minutes. Yields: 6 main servings.

Beefy Vegetable Soup

1½ pounds ground beef
1 medium onion, chopped
2 teaspoons minced garlic
1 (46 ounce) can V8® juice
2 cups coleslaw mix
1 (15 ounce) can stewed tomatoes
1 (6 ounce) package frozen corn
1 (16 ounce) package frozen mixed vegetables
2 tablespoons Worcestershire sauce
1 teaspoon dried basil

• Cook ground beef, onion and garlic in nonstick skillet until meat is no longer pink and drain. Transfer to 5-quart slow cooker. Stir in remaining ingredients. Cover and cook on HIGH for 4 to 5 hours.

The cattle industry is the largest job provider in agriculture. There are more than one million cattle operations in the U.S. There are 1,470,000 cattle in Illinois.

Minestrone Soup

This is great warmed the next day.
Leftovers never tasted so good.

**2 - 3 pounds beef chuck roast, arm roast or sirloin
steak**
1 medium onion, chopped
4 tablespoons olive oil
3 (10 ounce) cans beef broth
**2 (16 ounce) cans diced tomatoes with Italian herbs
and garlic**
1 teaspoon celery salt
1 tablespoon garlic powder
½ teaspoon thyme
½ teaspoon basil
½ teaspoon oregano
½ teaspoon rosemary
1½ cups macaroni shells
2 (15 ounce) cans mixed vegetables
1 (15 ounce) can dark red kidney beans, drained
1 (10 ounce) package chopped spinach, thawed

- Cut beef into ½-inch cubes. In heavy roasting pan brown beef cubes along with onion in olive oil until tender. Add 3 cups water, beef broth, diced tomatoes, bay leaf, celery salt, garlic powder, thyme, basil, oregano and rosemary. Bring to a boil. Reduce heat. Cover and simmer 1 hour.

- Add macaroni shells, uncooked, and simmer for additional 10 minutes. Add mixed vegetables, kidney beans and spinach and continue to simmer for another 10 minutes. Serve with hot Italian bread.

Oven-Baked Minestrone Soup

2 pounds stew beef, cubed
1 cup chopped onions
2 cloves garlic, minced
2 tablespoons olive oil
3 (14 ounce) cans beef broth
1 (16 ounce) can kidney beans
1 (14 ounce) can diced stewed tomatoes
1½ cups carrots, thinly sliced
1 (8 ounce) can whole pitted ripe olives
2 cups sliced elbow macaroni
½ teaspoon dried basil leaves
¼ teaspoon dried thyme leaves
¼ teaspoon dried oregano leaves
¼ teaspoon rosemary leaves
¼ teaspoon ground savory

- Preheat oven to 400°. In large, heavy, roasting pan, combine beef, onion, garlic, oil, 1 teaspoon each of salt and pepper and stir occasionally. Bake uncovered for 45 minutes.

- Leave soup in oven and reduce heat to 350°. Combine beef broth and 2¾ cups water in 2-quart microwave-safe dish. Microwave on HIGH for 10 minutes or until it begins to boil and add to beef mixture.

- Stir in beans, tomatoes, carrots and ripe olives. Cover and bake 2 hours or until meat is tender. Stir in zucchini, macaroni and herbs. Cover and bake 30 minutes or until vegetables are tender. Serve, sprinkled with parmesan cheese.

Chicken-Noodle Soup

2 (32 ounce) cartons low-salt chicken broth
1 (3½ pound) chicken, cut up or chicken pieces*
½ cup chopped onion
2 carrots, thinly sliced
2 ribs celery, sliced
2 tablespoons butter
1 cup quartered mushrooms
1 tablespoon fresh lemon juice
1 (8 ounces) package dried egg noodles

- Combine chicken broth and chicken in heavy large pot. Bring to a boil. Reduce heat, cover partially and simmer until chicken cooks through, about 20 minutes. Transfer to bowl.

- Cool chicken and broth. Discard skin and bones and cut chicken into bite-size pieces and set aside. Spoon fat from top of chicken broth and return to simmer.

- Add onion, carrots and celery. Simmer until vegetables are tender, about 8 minutes. Melt butter in heavy skillet over medium-high heat. Add mushrooms and saute until they begin to brown, about 5 minutes.

- Stir in lemon juice and pour into broth. Stir in noodles and chicken. Simmer until noodles are tender, about 5 minutes. Season soup with a little salt and pepper.

TIP: If you don't know how to cut up a chicken or if you know how, but just don't want to cut up chicken, buy your favorite pieces and get on with your day.

Turkey-Barley Tomato Soup

1 pound lean ground turkey
¾ cup sliced or baby carrots
1 medium onion, chopped
1 rib celery, chopped
1 clove garlic, minced
1 (1 ounce) envelope reduced-sodium taco seasoning, divided
1 (28 ounce) can Italian diced tomatoes with juice
¾ cup quick-cooking barley
⅛ teaspoon dried oregano

- In heavy roasting pan, cook turkey, carrots, onion, celery, garlic and 1 tablespoon taco seasoning over medium heat until meat is no longer pink. Stir in the 3½ cups water, tomatoes and remaining taco seasoning.

- Bring to a boil and reduce heat. Cover and simmer for 20 minutes. Add barley. Cover and simmer for 15 to 20 minutes longer or until barley is tender. Stir in oregano.

Illinois is ranked 13th for turkey production in the United States. Turkeys are the only breed of poultry native to the Western Hemisphere.

Cheesy Ham Chowder

10 bacon slices
1 large onion, chopped
1½ cups diced carrots
3 tablespoons all-purpose flour
3 cups milk
1 (14 ounce) can chicken broth
3 cups potatoes, cubed
1 (15 ounce) can whole kernel corn, drained
3 cups shredded cheddar cheese
3 cups fully-cooked ham, cubed

- In large soup pot, fry bacon until crisp, crumble and set aside. Saute onions and carrots in pan drippings. Stir in flour and gradually add milk and chicken broth. Bring to a boil. Cook and stir until mixture thickens. Add potatoes, corn and 1 teaspoon pepper. Reduce heat and simmer uncovered for 20 minutes. Add cheese and ham. Heat until cheese melts. Stir in bacon.

Creamy Corn Chowder

6 slices bacon, chopped
¼ cup chopped celery
¼ cup chopped onion
1¼ cups diced potatoes
3 cups corn
1 quart milk
2 eggs, hard-boiled eggs, chopped

- Saute bacon in roasting pan and add 2 cups water, celery, onion, potatoes and corn. Cook until vegetables are soft. Add milk, eggs and butter. Heat to boiling point and serve.

Baked-Bean Chili

2 pounds ground beef
1 (1 ounce) packet chili seasoning
2 (28 ounce) cans baked beans
1 (46 ounce) can V-8 juice

- Brown meat and drain. Transfer meat and remaining ingredients to slow cooker. Cook on LOW for 4 to 5 hours. Yields: 18 servings.

Stick-To-Your-Ribs White Chili

1 small onion, chopped
2 ribs celery, chopped
½ red pepper, chopped
1 clove garlic minced
3 tablespoons olive oil
3 (15 ounce) cans great northern beans
5 cups cooked, cubed chicken
2 teaspoons cumin
1 teaspoon oregano

- Mix all ingredients together. Bring to a boil and simmer for 10 to 15 minutes.

TIP: Garnish with shredded Monterey Jack cheese and 1 tablespoon of sour cream.

Turkey-Cabbage Stew

1 pound ground turkey
1 medium onion, chopped
3 cloves garlic, minced
1 tablespoon brown sugar
4 cups chopped cabbage
1 (28 ounce) can diced tomatoes
2 medium carrots, sliced
¼ teaspoon dried thyme
1 tablespoon vinegar
1 teaspoon dried oregano

- In large saucepan, cook turkey, onion and garlic over medium heat until meat is no longer pink. Drain. Add remaining ingredients. Bring to a boil. Cover and simmer for 6 to 8 minutes or until vegetables are tender. Yields: 6 servings.

Blue Ribbon Broccoli Salad

2 stalks broccoli
10 strips bacon, fried, crumbled
⅔ cup raisins
½ cup finely diced onions
2 teaspoons chopped nuts

Dressing:
1 cup mayonnaise
½ cup sugar
3 tablespoons vinegar

- Cut broccoli into florets and combine with bacon, raisins, onions and nuts. Mix dressing and pour over ingredients just before serving.

60

Colorful Cauliflower Salad

1 head cauliflower
2 green bell peppers, seeded
1 (2 ounce) jar diced pimentos, drained
1 (4 ounce) can sliced black olives, drained

Dressing:
⅓ cup vegetable oil
3 tablespoons red wine vinegar
3 tablespoons lemon juice
1 teaspoon sugar

- Cut cauliflower into medium sliced florets. Slice green peppers into thin strips. Toss all vegetables in salad bowl.

- Combine all dressing ingredients with salt to taste and ⅛ teaspoon pepper in jar and shake well. Pour over tossed vegetables and marinate at least 1 hour before serving.

There are 219,000 horses in Illinois, most of them are used for show or recreation. Horses belong to a group called equine or equus. A group of horses is a called a herd. There are more than 350 different breeds of horses and ponies.

Crunchy Tossed Salad

½ cup vegetable oil
¼ cup sugar
2 tablespoons vinegar
1 large head lettuce, sliced
6 bacon strips, cooked and crumbled
⅓ cup sliced almonds, toasted
¼ cup sesame seeds, toasted
¾ cup chow mein noodles

- Combine oil, sugar, vinegar and a little salt and pepper in jar with tight-fitting lid and shake well. Chill for 1 hour.

- Just before serving, combine lettuce, bacon, almonds and sesame seeds in large bowl. Add dressing and toss. Top with chow mein noodles.
  Yields: 12 servings.

Cucumber-Dill Salad

½ cup sour cream
¼ cup mayonnaise
1 tablespoon dill weed
2 tablespoons red onion, chopped
1 tablespoon vinegar
2 large cucumbers, sliced

- Mix sour cream, mayonnaise, dill weed, red onion and vinegar. Pour over cucumbers in large bowl and toss to coat. Sprinkle with ¼ teaspoon pepper.

Catalina-Spinach Salad

2 (10 ounce) packages fresh spinach, torn
2 large tomatoes, diced
2 (8 ounce) cans water chestnuts, drained
2 cups chow mein noodles
2 eggs, hard-boiled, chopped
12 strips bacon, fried, crumbled

Dressing:
½ cup vegetable oil
¼ cup ketchup
¼ cup red or white wine vinegar
¼ cup finely chopped onion
3 tablespoons sugar
2 teaspoons Worcestershire sauce

- Combine all salad ingredients in large bowl. Combine and mix dressing ingredients plus ½ teaspoon salt in jar and shake well. Pour dressing over salad and toss well. Serve immediately.

TIP: If you have a large crowd, just double this recipe. It's really something different!

Iowa, Illinois, Nebraska and Minnesota account for over 50 percent of the corn grown in the U.S. The majority of corn grown in Illinois is field corn, used for livestock feed.

Day-Before Vegetables

5 cups broccoli florets
4 cups thinly sliced cauliflower
1 medium green pepper, seeded, chopped
1 small red onion, thinly sliced
6 - 8 strips bacon, fully cooked, drained, crumbled

Dressing:
1 cup mayonnaise
½ cup vegetable oil
⅓ cup sugar
⅓ cup cider vinegar
1 teaspoon mustard

- Combine all vegetables and bacon in large bowl. Combine dressing ingredients with a little salt and pepper in separate bowl and whisk together. Pour dressing over vegetables and bacon. Serve cooled. Stir before serving.

TIP: This recipe can be made the day before and it will still be crisp.

An ear of corn averages 800 kernels in 16 rows. A pound of corn consists of approximately 1,300 kernels. Each corn kernel contains four major components: starch, protein, oil, and fiber.

Potato Salad

1 cup mayonnaise
2 tablespoons vinegar
5 medium, potatoes, cooked, peeled, cubed
1 cup thinly sliced celery
½ cup chopped onions
4 eggs, hard-boiled, chopped

- In large bowl, combine mayonnaise, vinegar, 1 teaspoon salt and 1 teaspoon pepper. Add potatoes. Stir in remaining ingredients and chill. Yields: 8 servings.

New Potato Salad
with Bacon and Mustard Seed

2 tablespoons mustard seeds
⅓ cup sherry wine vinegar
1 (16 ounce) package bacon, divided
3½ pounds new potatoes
⅔ cup olive oil
½ cup chopped fresh parsley

- Soak mustard seeds in vinegar for 1 hour. Fry about 12 ounces bacon in skillet until crisp, drain. Boil potatoes with 1 tablespoon salt until just tender. Drain and cool slightly.

- Quarter potatoes and toss with vinegar mixture and ½ teaspoon salt. Cool. Add remaining ingredients and season to taste with freshly ground pepper.

65

German Potato Salad

5 - 6 medium potatoes
1 pound bacon, cook, crumbled
½ - ¾ cup onion, chopped
½ cup flour
1¼ cups white vinegar
½ cup packed brown sugar
¼ cup sugar

- Boil potatoes whole until fork tender. Peel and slice. Reserve bacon grease. Combine onions with potatoes and bacon and set aside.

- Heat bacon grease, add flour and stir until bubbly. Stir in 2¼ cups water, vinegar and both sugars. Stir until smooth and slightly thick. Pour dressing over potatoes, bacon and onions; toss.

Sweet Potato Salad

2 pounds sweet potatoes, washed
1½ cups mayonnaise
2 teaspoons dijon-style mustard
4 eggs, hard-boiled, chopped
1½ cups minced celery
8 green onions, sliced

- Place sweet potatoes in large saucepan and cover with water and cook 35 minutes. Drain, cool, peel and cube.

- Mix mayonnaise and mustard in large bowl. Add eggs, celery, green onions and potatoes, stir gently. Chill before serving.

Marinated Vegetables

3 carrots, sliced in rounds
1½ cups broccoli florets
1½ cups cauliflower florets
1 cup sliced zucchini
1 cup sliced celery
4 green onions, sliced
1 (3 ounce) can sliced ripe olives, drained
1 (4 ounce) can sliced mushrooms, drained
Cherry tomatoes, halved
2 tablespoons chopped fresh parsley

Dressing
1 (1 ounce) packet dry original ranch dressing mix
⅔ cup salad oil
¼ cup vinegar

- Steam carrots over hot water for about 2 minutes. Add broccoli, cauliflower and zucchini. Continue to steam just until vegetables are tender-crisp. Transfer to large bowl and add celery, onions, olives and mushrooms.

- For dressing: combine dressing mix , salad oil and vinegar in jar and shake well. Pour over vegetables and toss. Refrigerate overnight. Add tomatoes and parsley just before serving.

Summer Corn Salad

1 (15 ounce) can white shoe-peg corn, drained
1 (15 ounce) can French-style green beans, drained
1 (15 ounce) can baby peas, drained
4 ribs celery, chopped
1 onion, chopped
1 green bell pepper, seeded, chopped

Dressing:
1 cup sugar or sweetener
½ cup salad oil
½ cup vinegar

- Place corn, green beans and baby peas in bowl. Add celery, onion, and green bell pepper. Combine dressing ingredients and pour over vegetables. Toss well. Refrigerate. Stir occasionally.

TIP: Salad keeps up to 2 weeks in refrigerator. If you want to have a fancy salad, you can add sliced water chestnuts and fresh mushroom caps.

Corn is America's number one field crop. More than half of U.S. corn is fed to livestock! Asia buys the most corn from the United States.

Sunny Broccoli-Cauliflower Toss

2 cups cauliflower florets
2 cups broccoli florets
½ cup raisins
¼ cup sliced green onions
¼ cup sunflower seeds
3 slices bacon, cooked, crumbled

Dressing:
½ cup mayonnaise or salad dressing
2 tablespoons sugar or Splenda
1 tablespoon cider vinegar

- Combine salad ingredients except sunflower seeds and crumbled bacon and toss lightly. Combine dressing ingredients and pour over salad. Toss to coat. Sprinkle sunflower seeds and crumbled bacon on top. Yields: 8½ cup servings, 190 calories per serving.

You will eat about 45 acres worth of corn in your lifetime. Americans today consume 17.3 billion quarts of popped popcorn each year. Corn is a major component in many food items like cereals, peanut butter, snack foods and soft drinks.

Layered BLT Salad

4 cups finely shredded lettuce
1½ cups chopped tomatoes
¼ cup bacon crumbles
4 slices bread, toasted, cubed
½ cup shredded cheddar cheese
½ cup Thousand Island dressing
¼ cup mayonnaise
1 teaspoon parsley flakes

- Layer lettuce, tomatoes, bacon, toast, and cheese in an 8 x 8-inch dish. Combine dressing, mayonnaise and parsley. Spread evenly over salad. Cover and refrigerate for at least 30 minutes.

Layered Lettuce Salad

1 head lettuce, torn
½ cup chopped celery
½ cup chopped green bell pepper
1 (16 ounce) box frozen peas
1 red onion, sliced and broken into rings
2 cups mayonnaise
2 teaspoons sugar
1 (8 ounce) package shredded cheese
½ pound cooked bacon, crumbled

- Layer ingredients in order listed in 9 x 13-inch glass dish. Cover and refrigerate overnight.

Pasta-Veggie Salad

1 (16 ounce) package mall shell macaroni
1 small cauliflower, chopped
1 bunch fresh broccoli, chopped
1 cucumber, peeled, diced
2 ribs celery, diced
4 carrots, shredded
1 small green pepper, chopped
1 onion, chopped

Dressing:
1 (14 ounce) can sweetened condensed milk
1 cup vinegar
2 cups mayonnaise

- Cook pasta according to package directions and cool. Add remaining vegetables. Combine dressing ingredients plus salt and pepper to taste and mix thoroughly. Add to pasta and vegetable mixture; toss. Chill well for best flavor.

TIP: You can add 2 cups shredded cheese, if you have it, for extra flavor.

Milk and milk products such as cheese, yogurt and ice cream contain calcium.
Calcium gives us strong bones.
Dairy products give us calcium plus nine other essential nutrients.

71

Spaghetti Salad

4 eggs
½ cup lemon juice
2 cups powdered sugar
1 (15 ounce) can crushed pineapple, drained
6 apples, cubed
2 cups boiled spaghetti, drained
1(8 ounce) carton whipped topping
Chopped nuts (optional)

- Beat eggs. Add lemon juice and powdered sugar and cook in saucepan over low heat until thick. Cool. Place pineapple, apples and spaghetti in large bowl. Add cooked mixture. Fold in whipped topping and nuts; chill.

Thunder and Lightening Salad

½ cup vinegar
¼ cup vegetable oil
½ cup sugar
2 cups chopped tomatoes
2 cups chopped green bell peppers
2 cups peeled, chopped cucumbers
1 large onion chopped

- In medium bowl, mix vinegar, oil, sugar, and a little salt until sugar dissolves. Add chopped vegetables to mixture, cover and chill several hours before serving.

Mediterranean Salad

This is excellent with chicken dishes.

¼ cup pine nuts
1 head romaine lettuce, torn
1 cup crumbled feta cheese
1 medium tomato, chopped
½ cup seedless green grapes
½ cup seedless halved green grapes
4 tablespoons bottled Italian dressing
4 tablespoons olive oil

- Cook pine nuts in small skillet over medium heat about 2 minutes or until light brown and stir constantly. Remove and set aside to cool.

- Toss pine nuts with romaine, feta, tomato and grapes in salad bowl. In small bowl, whisk Italian dressing, olive oil, a little salt and pepper. Drizzle over salad.

Sweet Cucumbers

7 cups peeled, thinly sliced cucumbers
2 cups sugar
1 cup diced onion
1 cup diced green pepper
1 cup vinegar
1 teaspoon celery salt

- Mix cucumbers with 1 teaspoon salt and water to cover and let rest for 1 hour. Drain cucumbers and set aside. Mix remaining ingredients. Pour over cucumbers and let stand in refrigerator at least overnight. Stir occasionally.

Fiesta-Bean Salad

1 cup white vinegar
2 cups sugar or Splenda
1 (15 ounce) can cut green beans, drained
1 (15 ounce) can wax beans, drained
1 (15 ounce) can lima beans, drained
1 (15 ounce) can kidney beans, drained
2 green peppers, cored, seeded
2 ribs celery, sliced
2 (4 ounce) cans pimento
2 cups thin sliced onion

• Bring vinegar, ½ cup water, sugar and 1 tablespoon salt to a boil in saucepan. Cool. Place rest of ingredients in bowl and add dressing. Chill. Let stand for 24 hours and serve.

Farm-Hand Taco Salad

1 pound ground beef
1 onion, chopped
1 (1 ounce) packet taco seasoning
1 head lettuce, torn
3 tomatoes, chopped
1 (8 ounce) package grated cheese
1 (8 ounce) bottle Catalina dressing
1 (10 ounce) package original corn chips

• Brown ground beef and onion over low heat; add taco seasoning. Set aside. Combine all remaining ingredients in large bowl and toss carefully. Mix with ground beef and serve immediately.

Chicken-Taco Salad

2 tablespoons olive oil
4 cups chopped, cooked chicken
4 teaspoons chili powder
1 teaspoon ground cumin, optional
1 (6 ounce) can tomato sauce
1 head lettuce, chopped
1 - 2 ripe avocados peeled, sliced
2 cups assorted chopped vegetables
Tortilla chips

Salad Dressing:
2 tablespoons lime juice
5 tablespoons oil
2 tablespoons finely chopped cilantro

- Heat olive oil, chicken, chili powder, ground cumin and tomato sauce and cook in large skillet until hot. Combine all salad ingredients. In large serving bowl, toss lettuce, avocados, vegetables, salad dressing and cooked chicken. Serve with tortilla chips.

Illinois has 2,367 chicken farms. Chickens raised for their meat are called broilers or fryers.

Creamy Coleslaw

½ cup mayonnaise
2 tablespoons milk
1 tablespoon white vinegar
¼ cup sugar
½ teaspoon seasoned salt
¼ teaspoon celery seed
1 (16 ounce) package coleslaw mix

- Combine all ingredients except coleslaw in measuring jar and stir well. Combine dressing with slaw mix in large bowl. Refrigerate at least 1 hour to blend flavors. Stir again before serving.

Broccoli-Cheese Slaw

6 cups chopped broccoli florets
10 slices bacon, fried, crumbled
1 medium red onion, chopped
1 (8 ounce) package shredded sharp cheddar

Dressing:
1 cup mayonnaise
½ cup sugar
4 tablespoons red wine vinegar

- Mix broccoli, bacon, onion and cheese. In separate bowl, mix mayonnaise, sugar and vinegar. Toss all together and chill.

Broccoli Slaw

1 (16 ounce) package broccoli slaw
2 (3 ounce) packages ramen oriental noodles,
   crumbled
½ cup slivered almonds
2 tablespoons dried parsley
4 green onions, chopped
¾ cup sunflower kernels

Dressing ingredients:
1 tablespoon sugar
½ cup vinegar
¾ cup oil
2 tablespoons soy sauce

- Place slaw, noodles (do not use seasoning packet), almonds, parsley, onions and sunflower kernels in large bowl. Season with pepper to taste. Combine dressing ingredients and pour over salad ingredients. Toss, chill and serve.

TIP: If you prefer coleslaw mix or shredded cabbage, use them instead of broccoli slaw. They are delicious too.

Did you know that most vegetable oil is actually soybean oil? The soybean is 80 percent meal and 20 percent oil. Soybeans are in sunscreen, lip balm, hand lotion, and other make-up products.

Siesta Pizza

1 (8 ounce) package crescent dinner rolls
1 (8 ounce) package cream cheese, softened
2 tablespoons sour cream
2 teaspoons dry taco seasoning mix
⅔ head lettuce, chopped
2 tomatoes, chopped
½ cup sliced black olives
1 (8 ounce) package Mexican-style shredded cheese

• Preheat oven to 350°. Place crescent rolls on sprayed pizza pan and pinch seams together. Bake for 10 to 12 minutes until golden brown.

• In medium bowl, beat together cream cheese, sour cream and taco seasoning and spread mixture over crust. Sprinkle vegetables and cheese on top.

Diabetic Veggie Salad Dressing

2 cups fat-free mayonnaise
2 cups skim milk
8 packages sweetener

• Mix all ingredients. Pour dressing over salad or vegetables.

Souffle Salad

1 (3 ounce) box lime gelatin
1 (3 ounce) box lemon gelatin
2 tablespoons vinegar
1 cup mayonnaise
1 (8 ounce) can crushed pineapple with juice
1 cup chopped celery
1 cup grated carrots
1 green bell pepper, chopped
1 cup cubed processed cheese

• Dissolve lime and lemon gelatins in 2 cups boiling water. Add vinegar, ½ teaspoon salt, and mayonnaise. Mix until blended.

• Drain pineapple into measuring cup and add enough water to equal 1 cup. Add pineapple juice to gelatin mixture and chill. When partially set, stir in vegetables and cheese. Chill until set.

Wonderful Watergate Salad

1 (20 ounce) can crushed pineapple with juice
1 (4 ounce) box instant pistachio pudding
1 (8 ounce) carton whipped topping
1 cup miniature marshmallows
½ cup chopped nuts

• Mix pineapple and pistachio pudding in serving bowl. Fold in whipped topping, marshmallows and nuts. Mix and chill.

Lemon Gelatin Salad

2 (3 ounce) boxes lemon gelatin
1 (8 ounce) can crushed pineapple with juice
3 bananas, sliced
1 (10 ounce) package miniature marshmallows

Topping:
1 egg, beaten
2 tablespoons flour
½ cup sugar
1 cup orange juice
1 (8 ounce) carton whipped topping

- In bowl, pour 3¼ cups boiling water over gelatin and stir to dissolve and cool. Add pineapple, banana slices and miniature marshmallows. Let rest.

- For topping mixture, beat egg in saucepan, add flour, sugar and orange juice. While stirring, cook until thick and cool. Fold in whipped topping. Spread topping mixture over gelatin and refrigerate.

A kernel of wheat, sometimes called the wheat berry, is the seed from which the wheat plant grows. A kernel, or seed of wheat, is smaller than our fingernails. A wheat head contains 50 to 75 kernels.

Orange Salad Bowl

8 cups salad greens
2 (11 ounce) cans mandarin oranges, drained
½ cup chopped pecans
1 small red onion, sliced into rings

Celery Seed Dressing:
½ cup sugar
⅓ cup vinegar
1 tablespoon celery seed
1 small onion, chopped
1 teaspoon dry mustard
1 cup olive oil

- Combine well washed greens with orange sections, pecans and onion rings in salad bowl. Mix all dressing ingredients well and toss half dressing (using more if needed) with greens just before serving. Yields: 8 servings.

TIP: The dressing yields 1⅓ cups and can be kept in a jar or bottle in the refrigerator for a few days.

To "harvest" means to remove wheat kernels from the wheat plant. A modern combine can harvest 1,000 bushels of wheat per hour.

Orange-Tapioca Gelatin Salad

2 (4 ounce) boxes tapioca pudding
1 (3 ounce) box orange gelatin
1 (8 ounce) carton whipped topping
1 (11 ounce) can mandarin oranges
  or 1 (15 ounce) can crushed pineapple, drained

- Mix pudding and gelatin in saucepan with 3 cups boiling water. Mix well and cook until boiling. Remove from heat and chill until almost set. Stir in whipped topping and chopped mandarin oranges or crushed pineapple and chill.

Aunt Leta's
Orange Gelatin Salad

1 (1 ounce) packet unflavored gelatin
1 (3 ounce) box orange gelatin
1 (8 ounce) can crushed pineapple with juice
1 (11 ounce) can mandarin oranges with juice
1 cup finely shredded carrots

- Pour 1½ cups water into saucepan. Sprinkle unflavored gelatin into 1½ cups water and let stand 5 minutes. Bring to a boil and pour over orange gelatin in bowl. Stir until it dissolves.

- Drain pineapple and mandarin oranges to get 1¾ cups fruit juice. Stir in fruit juice and chill until it slightly thickens. Stir in pineapple, oranges and carrots. Chill until firm.

Out-Of-This-World Orange Salad

1 (16 ounce) carton cottage cheese
1 (12 ounce) carton whipped topping
1 (3 ounce) box orange gelatin mix
2 (11 ounce) cans mandarin oranges, drained
1 (20 ounce) can pineapple, crushed or tidbits,
  drained
½ cup chopped walnuts, optional

- Process cottage cheese in blender until creamy. Mix whipped topping and cottage cheese. Add gelatin and mix well.

- Add mandarin oranges, pineapple and nuts if desired. Mix all ingredients well. Refrigerate for at least 4 hours.

Perky Pink Salad

1 (8 ounce) carton whipped topping
1 (20 ounce) can crushed pineapple, drained
1 cup marshmallows
1 cup chopped nuts
1 (20 ounce) can cherry pie filing
1 (14 ounce) can sweetened condensed milk
1 cup flaked coconut, optional

- Mix all ingredients and refrigerate for several hours.

83

Pineapple Gelatin Salad

1 (8 ounce) can crushed pineapple
1 (3 ounce) box cherry gelatin
1 (16 ounce) carton cottage cheese
1 (8 ounce) carton whipped topping

- Place pineapple in pan and heat until it begins to boil. Remove from heat and add cherry gelatin. Stir and cool. When cool add cottage cheese and fold in whipped topping. Mix well and spoon in oblong cake pan or glass dish and refrigerate.

Pineapple Surprise

1 (20 ounce) can crushed pineapple, drained
1 (12 ounce) carton whipped topping
½ cup lemon juice
½ cup chopped nuts
1 (14 ounce) can sweetened condensed milk

- Mix all ingredients and refrigerate for 1 to 2 hours.

Pink Champagne Salad

1 (8 ounce) package cream cheese, softened
¾ cup sugar
1 (20 ounce) can crushed pineapple, drained
**1 (10 ounce) package frozen sliced strawberries with
  juice**
2 bananas, quartered, sliced
1 (8 ounce) carton whipped topping
1 cup chopped nuts

• Whip together cream cheese and sugar. Add pineapple, strawberries, bananas and whipped topping. Mix and add nuts.

• Place in mold, salad bowl or 9 x 13-inch dish. Freeze until firm. Remove from freezer 30 minutes before serving. Slice and serve. Yields: 16 servings.

Apple Salad

6 cups diced apples with peel
1 cup diced celery
1 cup broken pecan pieces

Dressing:
2 eggs, beaten
½ cup sugar
2 tablespoons vinegar
2 teaspoons vanilla

• Combine apples, celery and pecans and set aside. Mix all ingredients for dressing except vanilla and cook thoroughly until thick. Add vanilla. Pour salad dressing and serve over lettuce.

Apple-Pineapple Salad

1 (8 ounce) can pineapple tidbits, drained
3 apples, chopped
½ cup sugar
1 (12 ounce) carton whipped topping
1 cup miniature marshmallows
½ teaspoon cinnamon

- Pour pineapple over apples and add sugar. Stir in whipped topping, marshmallows and cinnamon. Mix and refrigerate.

TIP: This salad is good with grapes and nuts if you want more ingredients.

Johnny Apple Salad

9 apples
Lemon juice
3 (8 ounce) packages cream cheese, softened
1 (16 ounce) box brown sugar
½ teaspoon vanilla
1 (10 ounce) package miniature marshmallows
Peanuts

- Core and chop apples. Sprinkle with lemon juice so they won't discolor. Beat together cream cheese, brown sugar and vanilla in serving bowl. Add apples and marshmallows and toss gently. Sprinkle peanuts on top.

Taffy Apple Salad

1 (8 ounce) can crushed pineapple with juice
1 tablespoon flour
¼ cup sugar
2 tablespoons cider vinegar
1 egg, beaten
4 cups chopped Granny Smith apples with peel
1 cup salted peanuts
1 (8 ounce) carton whipped topping

- Drain pineapple into saucepan over medium heat. Add flour, sugar, vinegar and egg, cook and stir for several minutes until sauce thickens. When sauce mixture cools, add whipped topping.

- In separate bowl, mix apples, peanuts and pineapple. Add whipped topping mixture to apple mixture. Chill and serve.

Apples contain as much fiber as a whole bowl of most popular cereals. Apples are rich in pectin which is known to reduce cholesterol. Apples contain vitamins A, C, B-6 and B-12, along with thiamin and niacin. A medium sized apple has 5 grams of fiber, 20 percent of the recommended daily allowance.

Strawberry Pretzel Salad

3 tablespoon plus 1 cup sugar
¾ cup butter, melted
2⅔ cups crushed pretzels
1 (8 ounce) cream cheese, softened
1 (12 ounce) carton whipped topping.
1 (6 ounce) box strawberry gelatin
1 pint strawberries or 1 (16 ounce) package frozen
strawberries

- Add 3 tablespoons sugar and melted butter to pretzel crumbs and pat into a 9 x 13-inch pan. Bake at 350° for 10 minutes. Cool.

- In mixing bowl, beat together cream cheese and 1 cup sugar. Fold in whipped topping and mix thoroughly. Combine 2½ cups boiling water with strawberry gelatin and stir to dissolve. Add 1 pint strawberries. Cool slightly if using fresh strawberries.

- Pour cream cheese filling onto crumb crust and top with gelatin and strawberries. Refrigerate overnight.

Stupendous Strawberry Salad

1 (12 ounce) carton whipped topping
1 - 2 pints fresh strawberries, washed
1 (14 ounce) can sweetened condensed milk
3 tablespoons lemon juice

- Combine all ingredients and chill overnight.

Cranberry-Waldorf Salad

2 cups (½ pound) fresh cranberries
3 cups miniature marshmallows
¾ cup sugar
2 cups tart apples with peel, diced
½ cup green grapes
½ cup chopped walnuts
½ cup whipping cream, whipped*

- Chop cranberries in blender and combine with marshmallows and sugar. Cover and chill overnight. Add apples, grapes, walnuts and ¼ teaspoon salt. Fold in whipped cream and chill for several hours.

TIP: For a time-saver, substitute 1 (8 ounce) carton whipped topping for real whipped cream.

Cranberry Salad

2 (3 ounce) boxes cherry gelatin
1 (16 ounce) can whole cranberries
½ cup apples, diced
½ cup celery, diced
1 (8 ounce) can crushed pineapple with juice
½ cup chopped pecans

- Dissolve gelatin in 2½ cups boiling water. Cool slightly. Stir in cranberries, apples, celery, pineapple and nuts. Turn into glass dish and chill until firm.

Apricot Salad

2 (20 ounce) cans crushed pineapple with juice
1 cup sugar
1 (6 ounce) box apricot gelatin
2 (8 ounce) packages cream cheese, softened
10 tablespoons milk
2 (8 ounce) cartons whipped topping

- Bring crushed pineapple and sugar to a boil in saucepan. Add apricot gelatin, stir well and set aside to cool. In large bowl, beat cream cheese and milk. Fold in whipped topping. Add cooled pineapple mixture and mix together.

- Pour in 9 x 13-inch dish and refrigerate.

TIP: You can use other gelatin flavors too, so pick you favorite. If you want to make less salad, cut recipe in half and use a 9 x 9-inch dish.

Fast Raspberry Gelatin

1 (6 ounce) box raspberry gelatin
2 (12 ounce) packages frozen raspberries
1 cup applesauce

- Add gelatin to 2 cups boiling water and stir until it dissolves well. Add frozen raspberries and applesauce. Mix and place in refrigerator. Salad sets up in about 20 to 30 minutes.

Ribbon Salad

2 (3 ounce) boxes lime flavor gelatin
1 (3 ounce) box lemon flavor gelatin
½ cup miniature marshmallows
1 cup pineapple juice
1 (8 ounce) package cream cheese, softened
1 (20 ounce) can crushed pineapple with juice
1 (8 ounce) carton whipped cream
1 cup mayonnaise
2 (3 ounce) boxes cherry flavor gelatin

- Dissolve lime gelatin in 2 cups hot water. Add 2 cups cold water. Pour into 14 x 10 x 2-inch pan. Chill until partly set.

- Dissolve lemon gelatin in 1 cup hot water in top of double boiler. Add marshmallows and stir to melt. Remove from heat.

- Add pineapple juice and cream cheese. Beat until it blends well, stir in pineapple and cool. Fold in whipped cream and mayonnaise. Chill until thick.

- Pour over lime gelatin and chill until almost set. Dissolve cherry gelatin in 2 cups hot water. Add 2 cups cold water. Chill until syrupy and pour over pineapple. Chill until firm.

Crystal Salad

1 (3 ounce) box lemon gelatin
½ cup chopped celery
½ cup chopped apples
½ cup pineapple tidbits
½ cup whipped topping
½ cup mayonnaise
½ cup miniature marshmallows

• Stir 1 cup boiling water in gelatin and stir until it dissolves.
  Add ½ cup cold water and stir. Let rest until it starts to
  gel and add celery, apples and pineapple. Stir well and
  fold in whipped topping, mayonnaise and marshmallows.
  Refrigerate, serve chilled.

Chocolate-Caramel Nut Salad

1 (16 ounce) package instant vanilla pudding mix
1 cup milk
1 (12 ounce) carton frozen whipped topping, thawed
6 apples, peeled, cored, chopped
6 (2.16 ounce) bars Snickers candy, chilled, sliced
¼ cup seedless grapes, optional

• Prepare pudding with milk. Blend with whipped topping.
  Add apples, candy bar slices and grapes. Mix and
  refrigerate until chilled.

THE FARM STAND
Soy
Vegetables

Soy Foods

Illinois farmers have a love affair with the soybean!

A soybean plant produces a light brown bean long referred to as the "miracle bean".

It starts as a green plant which grows to as much as 4.5 feet tall. The blooms yield pods containing 4 or 5 beans. Harvest comes when the plant is all brown and no growing can be found.

A machine called a combine is used to harvest the precious bean. From there they are trucked to an elevator for selling, storage and on to the processing plant.

Illinois farmers produced 47 bushels (60 pounds in 1 bushel) per acre (land the size of a football field) for a total of 444 million bushels in 2005.

In processing, soybeans are cleaned, cracked, hulled and rolled into flakes. This ruptures the oil cell for efficient extraction. The soybean oil finds its way into such products as margarine, salad dressings and cooking oils. The remaining flakes can be processed into edible soy-protein products or used to produce soybean meal for animal feeds.

Soy hulls are processed into fiber-bran breads, cereal and snacks. They are the highest natural source of dietary fiber. Further processing yields soy protein concentrate, textured protein, soy flour, etc.

Soy Health Claim

The Food and Drug Administration has ruled that a diet low in saturated fat and cholesterol that includes 25 grams soy protein a day may reduce the risk of heart disease. It is easier than you think to get the 25 grams. If you divide 25 by 4, you come up with 6.25, so with 4 servings of soy foods (like soy milk, a soy protein bar, soy nuts and soy-enriched cereal) you get 25 grams before you know it. There are many foods to choose from.

Nutrition

Soy protein is the only plant protein that contains the 8 essential amino acids. Soy is a good source of B vitamins, including folate. Some soy foods are very high in fiber, including edamame, dried soybeans, soy flour and textured vegetable protein. Soy contains linoleic acid and essential omega-3 fatty acids plus calcium and zinc. They contain phytochemicals that may help prevent chronic diseases.

Prevention or Treatment of Chronic Diseases

- *Heart Disease* – Most important is the health claim. Plus, soy may keep blood vessels healthy and help control blood pressure.
- *Cancer* – Soy contains at least five phytochemicals that may help prevent or slow the progression of some cancers.
- *Osteoporosis* – Soy may help in preventing bone loss and may minimalize symptoms of menopause.
- *Diabetes* – Soy foods may help keep blood glucose levels under control. Some soy foods may also reduce the risk of developing kidney disease.
- *Weight Control* – Soy is low in calories and high in nutrition. When soy is replaced with higher-fat foods, it reduces the overall fat content of the diet.

Soy – The Good Stuff

Soy is good for all age groups, from infant formula to old age. More information can be found from The SoyFood Association of North America on the Web at www.soyfoods.org and The Illinois Center for Soyfoods at www.soyfoodsillinois.uiuc.edu.

Spinach Dip

**1 (10 ounce) package frozen chopped spinach,
thawed, drained**
1 (1 ounce) package dry vegetable soup mix
1 (12 ounce) package firm silken tofu
1 (8 ounce) can water chestnuts, coarsely chopped
⅔ cup chopped green onions
1 cup low-fat sour cream
½ cup low-fat mayonnaise

- Combine all ingredients in large bowl until dip blends well.
  Cover and chill for 2 hours. Stir before serving. Makes
  about 4 cups.

Tofu Dip

**1 (12.3 ounce) package Mori-Nu Silken Tofu,
softened**
1 (1 ounce) packet ranch-style dressing mix
½ cup mayonnaise-type salad dressing

- Blend all ingredients in blender until smooth. Chill.
  Use with chips or vegetables for dipping.

*TIP: Firm or extra firm tofu can also be used. Pour in
teaspoon of milk if too thick.*

Easy-Day Vegetable Lasagna

8 green onions, chopped
1 cup sliced fresh mushrooms
1 tablespoon soy oil
1 (48 ounce) jar low-sodium, low-fat spaghetti sauce
½ (10 ounce) package low-fat firm silken tofu
1 (10 ounce) package frozen chopped spinach,
thawed, drained
1 egg, beaten
½ teaspoon garlic powder
½ teaspoon oregano
1 (8 ounce) package uncooked lasagna noodles
1 (8 ounce) package fat-free shredded mozzarella
cheese

- Preheat oven to 350°. Spray 9 x 13-inch baking pan
  with non-stick vegetable oil. Saute green onions and
  mushrooms in soy oil. Add spaghetti sauce and set aside.

- Combine tofu, spinach, egg, garlic powder, oregano, ½
  teaspoon salt and ¼ teaspoon pepper and mix well. In
  baking dish, spread a layer of spaghetti sauce, followed by
  half uncooked noodles, tofu mixture, remaining noodles
  and remaining sauce.

- Cover pan with aluminum foil. Bake 45 minutes. Remove
  foil and top with cheese. Bake, uncovered, for additional 15
  minutes. Allow to stand 10 minutes before serving. Yields:
  8 to 10 servings.

Tacos

1 pound tempeh, defrosted and cut into large chunks; or
1 pound tofu, crumbled; or 1 cup TVP rehydrated in 1 cup boiling water
2 tablespoons vegetable oil
1 packet taco seasoning
6 corn tortillas, warmed
1 can vegetarian refried beans, heated
Chopped tomatoes
Chopped lettuce
Chopped scallions
Salsa

- In large saucepan, place the tempeh chunks in oil. Crumble tempeh chunks with back of fork, cook tempeh (or tofu or TVP) over medium heat for about 10 minutes. Add taco seasoning and ½ cup water to saucepan; cook until sauce is thick and tempeh, tofu or TVP is completely coated.

- To serve, spread each tortilla with generous layer of refried beans. Add several heaping spoonfuls of tempeh, tofu or TVP. Sprinkle with chopped tomatoes, lettuce and scallions. Top with salsa. Yields: 6 tacos.

New Bean Salad

1 pound green beans, trimmed, cut into 1½-inch pieces
1½ cups frozen shelled green soybeans (edamame) available in health section of grocery   store
3 tablespoons extra virgin olive oil
¼ cup balsamic vinegar
¼ cup red wine vinegar
1 tablespoon sugar
1 (15 ounce) can black soybeans, drained, rinsed
1 small red onion, finely chopped

- Cook green beans for 5 minutes or until tender. Place frozen soybeans in colander and drain green beans over soybeans. Rinse with cold water until cool and drain well.

- In large bowl, whisk oil, vinegars, sugar and 1½ teaspoons salt and ¼ teaspoon pepper. Add black soybeans and onion and toss to coat. Let stand 1 hour and chill until ready to serve.

TIP: To save time, you can use 2 (15 ounce) cans cut drained green beans instead of fresh beans.

Decatur, Illinois is the soybean capital of the world. Soybeans are a major ingredient in hog feed. American livestock consume about 22.2 million tons of soybean meal a year.

Game-Day Pretzels

2½ cups all-purpose flour, divided
1¼ cups oats
1 cup soy flour
2 tablespoons sugar
1 (¼ ounce) package active dry yeast
¾ cup soy milk
2 tablespoons butter
1 egg, beaten
Kosher salt crystals to taste

- In large mixing bowl, combine 1 cup all-purpose flour with oats, soy flour, sugar, yeast and 1½ teaspoons salt and mix well. In small saucepan, heat soy milk, ¾ cup water and butter over low heat until hot. Add to flour mixture and beat 3 minutes. Stir in enough remaining flour to form soft dough that pulls away from sides of bowl.

- Knead on floured surface until smooth and elastic. Cover loosely with plastic wrap and let rise for 10 minutes. Divide dough into 24 pieces; roll each piece into 12-inch rope. Shape into pretzels or desired shapes.

- Place on lightly sprayed baking sheets, cover loosely with plastic and let rise for 10 minutes. Brush pretzels with beaten egg and coat with kosher salt. Bake at 350° for 15 to 20 minutes or until golden brown. Cool. Makes 24 pretzels.

Spicy Baked Beans

1 pound bulk hot sausage
1 medium green bell pepper, chopped
1 medium onion, chopped
1 (32 ounce) can pork and beans
1 (15 ounce) can black-eyed peas, drained, rinsed
1½ cups ketchup
1 (15 ounce) can kidney beans, drained, rinsed
1 (15 ounce) can pinto beans, drained, rinsed
¾ cup packed brown sugar
1 (15 ounce) can great northern beans, drained
2 teaspoons ground mustard

- In large skillet, brown sausage and drain. Add green pepper and onion and saute. Add remaining ingredients and mix well. Pour into sprayed 9 x 13-inch baking pan. Cover and bake at 325° for 1 hour. Uncover and bake an additional 25 minutes.

Barbecue Green Beans

1 small onion, chopped
3 strips bacon, cooked crisp, drained
¼ cup white sugar
¼ cup packed brown sugar
¼ cup vinegar
2 (15 ounce) cans green beans, drained

- Saute onions in 1 tablespoon bacon drippings. Combine sugars, vinegar, onions and bacon. Pour mixture over green beans in saucepan and cook over medium heat until bubbly.

Creole Green Beans

6 slices bacon
¾ cup chopped onion and green bell pepper
2 tablespoons brown sugar
2 tablespoons flour
1 tablespoon Worcestershire sauce
⅛ teaspoon dry mustard
1 (15 ounce) can stewed tomatoes
1 pound cooked fresh green beans

- Cook bacon until crisp. Remove from pan and saute onion and green bell pepper in bacon drippings. Blend in sugar, flour, Worcestershire sauce,
  ½ teaspoon salt, ¼ teaspoon pepper and dry mustard. Stir until smooth. Add tomatoes and beans and top with bacon.

Calico Beans

1 pound ground beef
2 large onions, chopped
½ pound bacon, chopped
1 (55 ounce) can baked beans
1 (15 ounce) can kidney beans, drained
2 (15 ounce) cans lima beans with liquid
½ cup ketchup
½ cup packed brown sugar
¼ cup molasses
1 tablespoon mustard

- In heavy pot, brown ground beef, onions and bacon. Add remaining ingredients and bake at 350° for 45 minutes. Makes 12 to 15 servings.

Brussel Sprouts with Celery

2 cups celery, thinly sliced
1 medium onion, sliced
3 tablespoons melted butter
3 tablespoons flour
1 teaspoon celery salt
1 (10 ounce) can chicken broth
2 (10 ounce) packages frozen brussel sprouts,
cooked, drain

- Saute celery and onion in butter in saucepan. Add flour and celery salt. Gradually add broth, cook over low heat and stir often. Add brussel sprouts, heat completely, but do not boil. Makes 6 to 8 servings.

Carrot Casserole

8 cups sliced carrots
2 medium onions, sliced
3 tablespoons butter
1 (10 ounce) condensed cream of celery soup
1 cup shredded cheddar cheese
1 cup seasoned croutons

- Place carrots in saucepan and cover with water. Bring to a boil and cook until tender-crisp. In skillet, saute onions in butter until tender. Stir in soup and cheese. Drain carrots and add to onion mixture.

- Pour into sprayed 9 x 13-inch baking dish and sprinkle with croutons. Bake uncovered at 350° for 25 minutes.

Corn Bake

1 (15 ounce) can whole kernel corn, drain half liquid
1 (15 ounce) can cream-style corn
1 (8 ounce) box cornbread mix
¾ cup vegetable oil
4 eggs
1⅓ cups shredded cheddar cheese, divided

- Preheat oven to 350°. Combine corn, cream-style corn, cornbread mix, oil, eggs and 1 cup cheese in medium bowl and pour into sprayed 9 x 13-inch baking pan. Top with ⅓ cup cheese and bake for 30 to 40 minutes. Insert toothpick in center. If it comes out clean, it is done.

TIP: If you prefer, you can substitute 3¾ cups "home" frozen corn instead of 2 cans of corn.

Easy Escalloped Corn Casserole

1 (15 ounce) can cream-style corn
1 (15 ounce) can whole kernel corn
1 cup cooked macaroni
¼ cup (½ stick) butter
1 (12 ounce) cubed processed cheese

- Combine all ingredients in 9 x 13-inch baking dish and bake at 350° for about 40 minutes. Stir once or twice while casserole bakes.

Corn Casserole

1 (15 ounce) can cream-style corn
1 (15 ounce) can whole kernel corn
1 (8 ounce) carton sour cream
½ cup (1 stick) butter, melted
1 (6 ounce) package cornbread mix

- Combine all ingredients in 9 x 13-inch baking dish and bake at 350° for 45 minutes to 1 hour.

Corn and Spinach Parmesan

¼ cup minced onion
4 tablespoons butter, divided
1 (15 ounce) can cream-style corn
1½ cups fresh spinach, chopped or 1 (15 ounce) can, drained
1 teaspoon vinegar
¼ cup fine breadcrumbs
2 tablespoons parmesan cheese

- Saute onion in 2 tablespoons butter in small skillet. Combine corn, spinach, vinegar, ½ teaspoon salt, ¼ teaspoon pepper and sauteed onions in medium bowl. Pour into lightly sprayed shallow baking dish.

- Blend breadcrumbs, parmesan cheese and 2 table-spoons melted butter. Sprinkle over vegetable mixture. Bake at 400° for 15 to 20 minutes or until bubbly and brown. Makes 6 to 8 servings.

Vegetable Casserole

1 (15 ounce) can French-style green beans, drained
1 (15 ounce) can wax beans, drained
2 cups tomato juice
½ cup sliced purple onion
1½ cups 2-inch carrot strips
2 cups 2-inch celery strips
¾ cup green bell pepper strips
4 tablespoons butter
1½ tablespoons sugar
3 tablespoons tapioca

- Combine all ingredients in covered 9 x 13-inch baking dish and mix well. Bake at 350° for 2 hours.
  Makes 10 to 12 servings.

Vidalia Casserole

4 - 5 Vidalia or sweet onions, sliced
¼ cup (½ stick) butter
¼ cup sour cream
¾ cup parmesan cheese
10 butter-flavored crackers, crushed

- In skillet, saute onions in butter over medium heat until tender. Remove from heat and stir in sour cream. Spoon half onions into sprayed 1-quart baking dish and sprinkle with cheese.

- Top with remaining onion mixture and sprinkle crackers on top. Bake at 350°, uncovered, for 20 to 25 minutes.

106

Wine Braised Red Cabbage

2½ cups thinly sliced red cabbage
½ cup peeled, chopped Granny Smith apples
¼ cup chopped red onion
2 tablespoons butter
¼ cup dry red wine
2 tablespoons red wine vinegar
½ cup peeled, finely grated russet potato
1 tablespoon honey

- In large, heavy skillet, saute cabbage, apples and onion in butter over medium heat until cabbage is tender. Add wine and vinegar, cover and cook until liquid evaporates. Add potato and honey, cover and cook until potato is tender.

Zucchini Squash Medley

3 cups zucchini squash, sliced
3 slices bacon, fried, chopped
4 cups chopped green bell peppers
1 small tomato, chopped
1 cup soft bread cubes
1 small onion, minced
¾ cup grated American cheese

- Cut zucchini squash into ¼-inch slices. Combine all ingredients except cheese in 1-quart baking dish. Sprinkle cheese on top and bake at 350° for 30 to 40 minutes.

Zucchini Puff

1½ cups zucchini, grated (about 2 medium zucchini)
3 tablespoons butter
⅓ cup onion, grated
¼ teaspoon thyme
2 eggs, separated
¼ cup milk
⅓ cup fine breadcrumbs, divided
¼ cup parmesan cheese, grated
1 tablespoon butter, melted

- Sprinkle zucchini generously with salt. Drain on paper towel, about 30 minutes. Press to remove excess water; pat dry. Melt butter in saucepan. Add onion. Cook until transparent. Remove from heat.

- Add thyme, beaten yolks, milk, ¼ cup breadcrumbs, and zucchini. Stir until mixed. Beat egg whites until stiff. Fold into zucchini mixture. Lightly spoon mixture into buttered 1-quart baking dish. Sprinkle with parmesan cheese, melted butter and remaining breadcrumbs.

- Bake at 325° for 25 to 30 minutes or until puffed and top is golden.

Wheat yields have improved by approximately one-half bushel per acre each year since 1900. A bushel of wheat weighs about 60 pounds. Wheat is used in bread, pasta, cereal, pretzels, and licorice.

Mushroom Stuffing

1 pound mushrooms, sliced
2 tablespoons butter, divided
1 cup chopped onion
1½ cups chopped celery
½ teaspoon poultry seasoning
½ cup chopped parsley
1 tablespoon grated orange peel
1 cup cooked rice

- Saute mushrooms in skillet with 1 tablespoon butter. Remove mushrooms from skillet. Melt remaining butter in skillet and cook onion and celery until tender-crisp. Combine all ingredients in 1½-quart baking dish. Cover and bake at 350° for 1 hour.

Veggie Pizza

2 (8 ounce) cans crescent rolls
2 (8 ounce) packages cream cheese, softened
1 teaspoon Worcestershire sauce
¼ teaspoon garlic salt
1 cup diced fresh tomatoes
1 cup chopped broccoli florets
½ cup chopped green bell pepper and onion
½ cup chopped mushrooms
1 (8 ounce) package shredded cheddar cheese

- Separate crescent roll dough into 4 rectangles and press into jellyroll pan. Prick with fork. Bake at 375° for 10 minutes until golden brown. Let cool. Beat together cream cheese, Worcestershire sauce and garlic salt until smooth and spread on crust. Add tomatoes, broccoli, bell pepper, onion and mushrooms. Sprinkle cheese over vegetables.

Sweet Potato Bake

2 eggs, separated
3 cups mashed sweet potatoes
1 cup sugar
1 teaspoon vanilla
½ cup milk
½ cup butter, melted

Topping:
⅓ cup flour
1 cup chopped pecans
⅓ cup butter, melted
1 cup packed brown sugar

- Beat egg yolks and mix sweet potatoes. Beat egg whites until fluffy and fold into potato mixture. Add sugar, vanilla, milk and butter.

- Pour into 9 x 13-inch baking dish. Combine topping ingredients in small bowl and sprinkle over top. Bake at 350° for 30 to 40 minutes.

Onion-Roasted Potatoes

1 (1 ounce) packet dry onion soup mix
4 medium all-purpose potatoes, cubed
⅓ cup olive oil

- Preheat oven to 425°. In 9 x 13-inch baking pan, combine all ingredients until evenly coated. Bake, uncovered and stir occasionally, about 35 minutes or until potatoes are tender and golden brown.

Omaha-Style Potatoes

1 (32 ounce) package frozen hash brown potatoes, thawed
½ cup diced onion
1½ cups grated cheddar cheese, divided
1 (10 ounce) can cream of celery soup
1 (10 ounce) can cream of potato soup
1 (8 ounce) carton sour cream
½ cup (1 stick) butter, sliced

- Place potatoes in 9 x 13-inch baking dish. Cover with onions, cheese and salt and pepper to taste. Combine soups and sour cream and pour over potatoes. Top with butter slices. Bake at 325° for 1 hour. Sprinkle remaining cheese on top.

Spanish Tomato Rice

8 slices of bacon
1 cup finely chopped onion
½ cup chopped green bell pepper
1 (15 ounce) can diced tomatoes
½ cup chili sauce
½ teaspoon Worcestershire sauce
1 teaspoon brown sugar
¾ cup uncooked long-grain rice

- Cook bacon in large skillet until crisp; drain half of drippings. In remaining drippings, cook onion and green pepper until tender but not brown. Add remaining ingredients plus 1½ cups water. Cover, simmer for 35 minutes. Crumble bacon on top.

Macaroni and Cheese

2 cups elbow macaroni, uncooked
½ cup (1 stick) butter, melted
¾ cup shredded cheddar cheese
¾ cup cubed processed cheese
½ cup shredded mozzarella cheese
5 cups milk

- Preheat oven to 350°. Mix all ingredients in large bowl. Pour into greased 9 x 13-inch pan and bake for 45 minutes. Cover with foil and bake additional 15 minutes.

Noodles

8 whole eggs
4 egg yolks
Flour

- Beat whole eggs, egg yolks, 2 tablespoons water and 1 teaspoon salt well. Add enough flour to form stiff ball. Roll out on floured board.

- Let dry to cutting consistency and cut into thin strips. Spread out on cookie sheets to dry, usually overnight. Freezes well.

GATHER ROUND
THE TABLE
Main Dishes

Chicken-Broccoli Bake

1 (10 ounce) can cream of chicken soup
⅓ cup mayonnaise
1 tablespoon lemon juice
½ cup cottage cheese
3 cups cooked chicken, cut up
1 (16 ounce) package frozen broccoli florets, thawed
1 cup grated cheddar cheese
1 cup seasoned breadcrumbs

- Preheat oven to 350°. Mix soup, mayonnaise, lemon juice and cottage cheese. Set aside. Place layer of half the chicken in sprayed 9 x 13-inch pan, a layer of half broccoli and end with half soup mixture. Repeat layers. Sprinkle cheddar cheese and breadcrumbs over top. Bake at 350° for 30 minutes or until thoroughly hot.

Chicken-Macaroni Casserole

1¼ cups uncooked macaroni
1 (10 ounce) can cream of mushroom soup
½ cup milk
1 tablespoon dried parsley
1 cup shredded, sharp cheddar cheese
2 cups cooked, cubed chicken

- Preheat oven to 400°. Cook macaroni according to package directions. Combine macaroni with remaining ingredients, but save enough cheese to sprinkle on top. Put in greased, 2-quart baking dish, cover and bake about 20 minutes.

Chicken Casserole

11 slices white bread, crust removed
4 cups cooked diced chicken
1 (4 ounce) can sliced mushrooms
1 (8 ounce) can dried, sliced water chestnuts
1 cup shredded sharp cheddar cheese
2 (10 ounce) cans celery soup
1 (4 ounce) can chopped pimento
4 eggs, well beaten
2 cups milk
2 cups buttered seasoned croutons

- Spray 9 x 13-inch baking pan and line with bread. Layer chicken, mushrooms and water chestnuts. Mix cheese, soup, pimentos, eggs and milk and pour over layers. Bake covered at 350° for 1 hour. Sprinkle croutons over top and bake uncovered 20 minutes.

Curried-Chicken Casserole

½ cup chopped onions and celery
¼ cup (½ stick) butter
2 cups cooked, cubed chicken
1 (10 ounce) can cream of mushroom soup
1 (10 ounce) can cream of chicken soup
1 (10 ounce) can chicken broth
1 cup milk
1 teaspoon curry powder
¾ cup instant rice

- Saute onion and celery in butter, add remaining ingredients and place in greased baking dish. Cover and bake 1 hour at 350°. Serve hot.

Chicken Divan

2 (10 ounce) cans cream of chicken soup
1 teaspoon lemon juice
1 teaspoon curry powder
¾ cup shredded cheddar cheese
½ cup mayonnaise
6 tablespoons (¾ stick) butter, melted
6 cups good white bread, cubed
1 (16 ounce) package frozen chopped broccoli,
  cooked
1 pound boneless, skinless chicken breast halves,
  cooked, cubed

- Preheat oven to 350°. Mix soup, lemon juice, curry, cheese and mayonnaise in separate dish. Toss melted butter with bread cubes.

- In buttered 9 x 13-inch pan, layer broccoli on bottom, then chicken, then soup mixture on top of that. Top dish with buttered bread cubes and cover with foil.

- Bake for 45 minutes. Take foil off and bake additional 15 minutes to brown bread cubes.

TIP: You can make this in 2 (8 x 8-inch) pans and freeze one pan. You can also make this the day before you bake it.

Delicious Hot Chicken Salad

4 - 6 chicken breasts, boiled, shredded
1 (10 ounce) can cream of chicken soup
1 (10 ounce) can cream of mushroom soup
1 cup real mayonnaise
1 (8 ounce) carton sour cream
½ cup chopped onions
3 eggs, hard-boiled, chopped
1 (8 ounce) can water chestnuts, sliced, optional
½ cup almond slices
1 (8 ounce) package shredded cheddar cheese
1 (3 ounce) can french-fried onions

- Preheat oven to 350°. Lay chicken in bottom of sprayed 9 x 13-inch baking dish. In mixing bowl, combine both soups, mayonnaise, sour cream, onions, eggs, water chestnuts and almonds.

- Pour mixture over chicken. Cover with cheese. Bake for 35 to 40 minutes. During last 15 minutes, cover with french-fried onions.

Each year, a person will eat approximately 250 eggs. A female chicken raised for eggs is called a laying hen. A hen requires 24 to 26 hours to produce an egg. Eggs contain the highest quality food protein known.

Layered-Chicken Casserole

6 - 8 slices bread
4 cups cooked, diced chicken
1 (8 ounce) fresh sliced mushrooms
3 tablespoons butter, divided
1 (8 ounce) can sliced water chestnuts, chopped, drained
½ cup mayonnaise
6 ounces muenster cheese slices
4 ounces American cheese slices
1½ cups milk
3 eggs beaten
1 (10 ounce) can cream of chicken soup
1½ cups breadcrumbs

- Preheat oven to 350°. Grease 9 x 13-inch pan. Place bread slices in to fit bottom of pan. Put diced chicken over bread. Saute mushrooms in 2 tablespoons butter and spread over chicken.

- Mix water chestnuts with mayonnaise and spread over mushrooms. Layer muenster and American cheese over water chestnuts.

- Mix milk, eggs and chicken soup and pour over all layers. Bake at 350 degrees for 60 to 70 minutes. Toss breadcrumbs with 1 tablespoon melted butter and sprinkle over top of casserole. Bake 10 minutes longer.

Tasty Turkey Tetrazzini

1 (8 ounce) package thin spaghetti
1 small onion, chopped
2 tablespoons butter
3 tablespoons flour
1 teaspoon dry mustard
1 (12 ounce) can evaporated milk
1 (14 ounce) can turkey broth
1 (4 ounce) can diced pimento
3 cups cooked diced turkey
¼ cup grated parmesan cheese

- Cook and drain spaghetti. Saute onion in butter. Remove from heat. Blend flour, 1 teaspoon salt, mustard and ¼ teaspoon pepper slowly.

- Stir in evaporated milk and turkey broth. Cook, stir until thick and boil 1 minute. Stir in pimento and mix with turkey and spaghetti. Put in buttered 9 x 13-inch pan. Cover and bake for 30 minutes at 375°. Sprinkle with parmesan cheese over top and bake another 5 minutes. Yields: 10 to 12 servings.

The male turkey is called a Tom. The female turkey is called a Hen. Baby turkeys are called Poults and are tan and brown. Turkeys will have 3,500 feathers at maturity.

119

Tasty Chicken Casserole

1 (12 ounce) package favorite pasta
1 (10 ounce) can mushroom soup
1 (10 ounce) can cream of celery soup
1 chicken, cooked, cut in bite-size pieces
1 (8 ounce) package cubed processed cheese
1 small onion, diced
½ cup chopped celery
1 (8 ounce) can green peas, drained
3 eggs, hard-boiled, chopped
1 (1 pint) carton half-and-half cream

- Preheat oven to 350°. Mix all ingredients into large bowl. Pour into sprayed, 9 x 13-inch baking dish. Cover and chill in refrigerator overnight. Bake at 350° for 1 hour.

Chicken and Dumplings

1 chicken
6 chicken bouillon cubes
3 cups flour
4 eggs
⅔ cup shortening

- Cut and boil chicken. Take chicken off bone. Put chicken and bouillon cubes back in pan with broth.
  If broth is not rich enough, add 1 stick butter.

- Mix remaining ingredients. Roll dumpling dough out very thin. Cut in strips and drop in broth. Add few drops yellow food coloring in broth. Cook until dumplings are tender. Yields: 4½ to 5 quarts.

Glorified Beef Casserole

1½ pounds ground beef
2 medium onions, chopped
1 cup sour cream
1 (10 ounce) can cream of chicken soup
1 cup seasoned breadcrumbs
1 (15 ounce) can whole kernel corn, drained
1 (10 ounce) can cream of mushroom soup
¾ cup noodles cooked, drained

- Preheat oven to 350°. Brown meat, season with ¾ teaspoon salt and ¼ teaspoon pepper and drain. Add onion and remaining ingredients except noodles and mix well. Add noodles, pour into buttered baking dish and cover with breadcrumbs. Bake until it bubbles.

Thrifty Beef-Noodle Casserole

1 (12 ounce) package noodles
1 pound ground beef, browned, drained
1 onion chopped
1 (10 ounce) can cream of mushroom soup
½ soup can milk
1 (10 ounce) can cream of chicken soup
1 (10 ounce) can cream of tomato soup

- Preheat oven to 325°. Cook noodles according to package directions. Brown beef and onion in skillet. Mix remaining ingredients and pour into sprayed 3-quart baking dish. Bake for 25 to 30 minutes.

Harvest Ground Beef Casserole

1 pound ground beef
1 cup chopped onion
1 (28 ounce) can diced tomatoes with liquid
1 tablespoon Worcestershire sauce
2 cups peeled, cubed potatoes
⅓ cup all-purpose flour
1 (10 ounce) package frozen corn, thawed
1 (10 ounce) package frozen lima beans, thawed
1 green pepper, seeded, cut into strips
1½ cups shredded reduced-fat cheddar cheese

- Preheat oven to 375°. In skillet, brown beef and drain. Add onion, tomatoes and Worcestershire sauce. Spoon into sprayed 3-quart baking dish. Layer with potatoes, flour, corn, lima beans and green pepper.

- Cover and bake for 1 hour 15 minutes. Sprinkle with cheese, cover and let stand until cheese melts.

Many medicines, including insulin, are made from the glands of the cow. Beef is a good source of B-vitamins, which helps promote healthy skin.

Chili-Upside-Down Casserole

1 pound ground beef
⅓ cup chopped onion
1 tablespoon shortening
1 (15 ounce) can chili beans with liquid
¼ teaspoon chili powder
1 teaspoon Worcestershire sauce
1 cup cooked tomatoes

Cornbread Batter:
1 cup flour
1 cup cornmeal
1 cup milk
2 teaspoons baking powder
¼ cup sugar
1 egg
1 heaping tablespoon butter, melted

- Preheat oven to 425°. Combine beef, onion and shortening. Saute until brown and drain. Add chili beans, chili powder, ½ teaspoon salt and tomatoes. Simmer for 30 minutes.

- Turn into buttered 9 x 13-inch baking dish. Mix all ingredients for cornbread batter plus ½ teaspoon salt and spread over casserole. Bake for 20 minutes.

Beef is a good source of ZIP (Zinc, Iron & Protein). Zinc, one of the minerals found in beef, is used for growth and fighting off illnesses.

Favorite Tater Tot Casserole

1½ pounds ground beef
2 (15 ounce) cans mixed vegetables, drained
2 (10 ounce) cans cream of chicken soup
1 (18 ounce) package frozen tater tots, thawed

- Preheat oven to 350°. Brown and drain hamburger and add salt and pepper to taste. Place in bottom of 9 x 13-inch baking pan. Add layer of mixed vegetables, chicken soup and tater tots.

- Bake for 1 to 1½ hours or until tater tops are golden brown.

TIP: If you don't want to use mixed vegetables, substitute your favorite vegetable.

Taco Tot Casserole

1 pound lean ground beef, browned, drained
1 (1.25 ounce) packet taco seasoning mix
1 (15 ounce) can whole kernel corn, drained
1 (11 ounce) can condensed nacho cheese soup
4 cups frozen tater tots, thawed

- Preheat oven to 375°. Brown beef and drain fat. Stir in taco seasoning mix. Put beef in ungreased 9 x 9-inch baking dish. Spoon corn over beef.

- Spoon nacho cheese over corn and arrange tater tots in single layer. Bake for 40 to 50 minutes. Serve with sour cream and salsa, if desired.

Mushroom Pizza Casserole

1 pound ground beef
2 (8 ounce) cans pizza sauce
2 (4 ounce) cans mushrooms with liquid
1 tablespoon dried oregano
1 teaspoon garlic salt
2 cups cooked macaroni or rotini
⅔ cup milk
1 (8 ounce) package shredded mozzarella cheese

- Preheat oven to 350°. In skillet brown ground beef and drain. Stir in pizza sauce, mushrooms with liquid, oregano and garlic salt. Bring to boil. Remove from heat.

- Combine pasta and milk.

- In sprayed 2-quart baking dish, layer half each of meat mixture, pasta and cheese. Repeat layers. Bake covered at 350° for 25 to 30 minutes.

TIP: If you want a garnish, try salami, cherry tomatoes and parsley.

A steer is a male that is raised for meat like hamburgers and steaks. A heifer is a young female that has not had a calf. A calf weighs about 80 pounds at birth. Cattle live an average of 9 to 12 years.

Pizza Casserole

1 pound ground beef
1 large onion, chopped
1½ cups uncooked elbow macaroni
1 (15 ounce) jar pizza sauce
1 (12 count) pepperoni slices
1 (8 ounce) package shredded mozzarella cheese

• Preheat oven to 350°. Brown beef with onion and drain. Bring 3 to 4 quarts water to boil in large pan, add macaroni and boil, uncovered for 10 to 12 minutes. Drain well.

• Mix pizza sauce with macaroni and ground beef. Place in sprayed 8 x 8-inch baking dish, alternating layers with pepperoni and cheese, ending up with cheese. Bake uncovered for 30 to 40 minutes.

Cattle eat and clean up cornstalks and cobs left in fields after harvesting the corn crop. Cattle scatter seeds, trim wild grasses, and aerate the soil with their hooves. Cows can eat around 40 pounds of food each day.

Wild Rice and Round Steak Casserole

1 pound round steak, cubed
1 large onion, chopped
1 (6 ounce) box long-grain and wild rice
1 (10 ounce) can cream of chicken soup
1 (10 ounce) can cream of mushroom soup
1 (4 ounce) can mushrooms
Garlic salt
Onion salt
Parmesan cheese

- Preheat oven to 350°. Brown round steak and onion. Add rice mixture (minus the seasonings). Add cream of chicken and cream of mushroom soup, 1 soup can water and mushrooms.

- Add seasonings and salt and pepper to taste. Put in baking dish and sprinkle with grated parmesan cheese on top. Bake at 325° for 1½ hours.

The first cow in America arrived in Jamestown colony in 1611.

127

Mexican Casserole

1 pound ground beef
1 medium onion, chopped
1 tablespoon chili powder
10 corn tortillas chips, broken
1 (15 ounce) can chili beans
1 (10 ounce) can tomatoes and green chilies
1 (10 ounce) can cream of chicken soup
½ cup shredded cheddar cheese

• Preheat oven to 350°. Brown ground beef and drain. Add onion and chili powder. Layer meat mixture, chips, beans, tomatoes and green chilies and chicken soup in baking dish. Top with cheese and bake at 350° until it bubbles.

Best Beef Stroganoff

1½ pounds round steak
¼ cup flour
¼ cup (½ stick) butter
1 (4 ounce) jar sliced mushrooms
½ cup chopped onion
1 small garlic clove, minced
1 (10 ounce) can concentrated beef broth
1 (8 ounce) carton sour cream
3 cups cooked noodles

• Cut steak in thin strips. Dust in flour. Brown in butter. Add mushrooms, onion and garlic. Brown lightly. Stir in beef broth. Cover. Cook 1 hour or until tender, stirring occasionally. Gradually stir in sour cream. Cook over low heat for 5 minutes. Serve over cooked noodles. Yields: 4 servings.

Sour Cream Noodle Bake

1 (8 ounce) package medium egg noodles
1 pound ground beef
¼ teaspoon garlic salt
1 (8 ounce) can tomato sauce
1 cup cottage cheese
1 (8 ounce) carton sour cream
1 cup onion, chopped
1 cup shredded cheddar cheese

- Cook noodles according to package directions, rinse in cold water and drain. Brown beef over medium heat and drain. Add 1 teaspoon salt, ⅛ teaspoon pepper, garlic salt and tomato sauce. Simmer 5 minutes.

- Combine cottage cheese, sour cream, onion and noodles. Alternate layers of noodle mixture and meat mixture in greased 2-quart baking dish. Top with cheese. Bake at 350° for 20 to 25 minutes.

Beef fat, called tallow, is an ingredient in soaps, cosmetics, candles, shortenings, and chewing gum.

129

Hungarian Beef and Rice

1 pound round steak, trimmed, thinly sliced
½ cup chopped onion
1 garlic clove, minced
⅓ cup ketchup
2 tablespoons brown sugar
2 tablespoons Worcestershire sauce
1 tablespoon brown mustard
1 teaspoon paprika
1 teaspoon cornstarch
Rice

- Saute steak strips, a few pieces at a time, until all brown. Add onion and garlic; saute 3 to 5 minutes. Stir in ½ cup water, ketchup, brown sugar, Worcestershire sauce, mustard, paprika and 1 teaspoon salt. Cover and simmer 20 minutes.

- Combine cornstarch with ¼ cup water. Stir into meat mixture. Heat and stir until shiny and thick. Serve over hot, fluffy rice. Yields: 2 servings.

Disneyland in California sells 4 million hamburgers per year. Each year, the average American eats 112 pounds of beef.

Baked Spaghetti

1 pound ground beef
1 cup chopped onion
1 (12 ounce) spaghetti, cooked, drained
2 (28 ounce) cans diced Italian tomatoes
1 (4 ounce) can mushrooms, stems and pieces,
  drained
1 (4 ounce) can sliced ripe olives, drained
2 teaspoons Italian seasoning or oregano
1 (8 ounce) package shredded cheddar cheese, divided

- Brown ground beef and onion while bringing water to boil for spaghetti. (A few drops of vegetable oil in water helps prevent spaghetti from sticking.) Drain beef and onion mixture.

- Add tomatoes, mushrooms, olives, seasoning and heat. Spread half of cooked spaghetti in sprayed 9 x 13-inch baking dish. Layer half beef mixture and sprinkle 1 cup shredded cheese on top. Repeat spaghetti, meat mixture and cheese layers. Bake at 350° for 30 to 35 minutes.

TIP: This recipe is great to make in advance. If chilled from refrigerator, then bake for 40 to 45 minutes.

Baked Lasagna

Meat Mixture:
2 pounds ground beef
1 medium onion, chopped
2 (6 ounce) cans tomato sauce
1 clove garlic, minced
1 teaspoon oregano
1 (12 ounce) box lasagna noodles

Cheese Mixture:
1 (16 ounce) carton small curd cheese
⅓ cup grated parmesan cheese
2 eggs beaten
1 (16 ounce) package shredded mozzarella cheese

- Brown ground beef and onion and drain excess grease. Add tomato sauce and garlic. Simmer 15 minutes. Add oregano, salt and pepper to taste.

- Cook noodles in boiling, salt water and drain. Place layer of noodles into sprayed 9 x 13-inch baking dish. Top with half meat mixture. Top with half cheese mixture. Sprinkle with half mozzarella cheese.

- Top with another layer of noodles, meat, cheese mixture and mozzarella cheese. Bake at 375° for 45 minutes.

Meatballs

¼ cup (½ stick) butter
2 pounds ground beef
1 egg
¾ cup milk
½ cup minced onion
¾ cup crushed crackers
⅛ teaspoon nutmeg

- Melt butter in 350° Dutch oven. Mix beef, egg, milk, onion, crackers, nutmeg plus 1½ teaspoons salt and ¼ teaspoon pepper and shape into 1-inch balls. Brown meatballs in melted butter and turn about 20 minutes into cooking time. Finish cooking. Top with barbecue sauce or cranberry sauce

Barbecue Sauce:
3 cups packed brown sugar
2 cups ketchup
1 teaspoon chili powder
1 teaspoon mustard
1 teaspoon Worcestershire sauce

- Mix all ingredients with 1 teaspoon salt and heat. Pour over meatballs, warm and serve.

Cranberry Sauce:
1 (16 ounce) can jellied cranberry sauce
3 tablespoons brown sugar
1 tablespoon lemon juice
1 cup ketchup

- Heat all ingredients thin enough to pour. Pour over meatballs and serve.

Marvelous Meat Loaf

¾ cup ketchup, divided
2 pounds ground beef
2 eggs, beaten
⅔ cup quick-cooking oats
¼ cup chopped onion
¼ cup green pepper, chopped
1 teaspoon seasoned salt
½ teaspoon garlic powder

- Preheat oven to 350°. Reserve ¼ cup ketchup for later use. Combine ground beef, eggs, oats, onion, green pepper, seasoned salt, ½ teaspoon black pepper, garlic and ½ cup ketchup. Shape into loaf. Bake for 45 minutes. Uncover, spread remaining ¼ cup ketchup on top of meat loaf and bake uncovered additional 15 minutes.

German Meatloaf

2 cups dry breadcrumbs
1 (15 ounce) can sauerkraut, drained
½ cup milk
½ cup chopped onions
3 eggs
2 tablespoons chili sauce or ketchup
2 pounds ground beef

- Preheat oven to 350°. Mix all ingredients except ground beef in large bowl. Stir in ground beef and 1 teaspoon pepper and mix well. Form into loaf shape and bake for 1 hour 15 minutes.

TIP: It takes about 8 slices of bread to equal 2 cups.

Porcupine Meatballs

1 pound ground beef
1 teaspoon baking powder
¾ cup milk
½ cup minute rice
1 (10 ounce) can tomato soup

- Preheat oven to 350°. Mix ground beef, baking powder, milk and rice; form into balls. Place into 9-inch, deep, baking dish. Pour soup over meatballs. Bake for 1 to 1½ hours. Yields: 6 servings.

Sweet-and-Sour Meat Loaf

1½ pounds ground beef
1 cup dry breadcrumbs
2 eggs, beaten
1 teaspoon instant minced onion
1 (15 ounce) can tomato sauce, divided

Topping:
2 tablespoons brown sugar
2 tablespoons vinegar
½ cup sugar
2 teaspoons prepared mustard

- Preheat oven to 350°. Mix beef, breadcrumbs and eggs. Add onion and half of tomato sauce. Form into loaf and place in 9 x 5 x 3-inch pan. Bake for 50 minutes. In saucepan, combine topping ingredients. Bring to boil. Drain juice from cooked meatloaf and pour topping over loaf. Bake 10 minutes more. Slice meat loaf and pour remaining tomato sauce over slices to serve.

Prime Rib and Au Jus

1 (3 - 4 pound) rib roast
Worcestershire sauce
1½ teaspoons garlic powder
1½ teaspoons crushed thyme

- Let roast sit at room temperature 1 hour. Poke fat at 1-inch intervals with fork. Rub top and sides with Worcestershire sauce. Mix garlic powder, crushed thyme, 1½ tablespoons salt and 1 teaspoon pepper and rub on exposed surfaces.

- Preheat oven to 350°. Place fat-side up in roasting pan. Bake for about 1½ to 2 hours. Use meat thermometer. Place in warm draft-free area while preparing Au Jus.

TIP: Plan on ½ pound per person. Cook about 25 to 3 0 minutes per pound.

Au Jus:
½ cup chopped onions
½ cup chopped carrots
½ cup chopped celery
1 tablespoon drippings from roast
¾ cup red wine
3 cups beef broth
2 small cloves garlic
½ teaspoon thyme

- Cook onions, carrots and celery in pan drippings over medium heat for 5 minutes. Add wine. Simmer about 10 minutes and reduce by two-thirds.

- Add beef broth, garlic and thyme. Simmer for 10 minutes. Strain and serve with meat.

Italian Sirloin-Tip Roast

1 (5 pound) sirloin tip roast
1 large onion, cut into wedges
1 large red bell pepper, seeded, sliced
1 large yellow bell pepper, seeded, sliced
1 tablespoon seasoned salt
2 tablespoons garlic powder
3 tablespoons Italian seasoning
1 tablespoon crushed, dried oregano
1 tablespoon crushed, dried rosemary
1 (14 ounce) can beef broth
¼ - ½ cup cornstarch

- Preheat oven to 325°. Place roast in Dutch oven. Surround with onion and peppers. Sprinkle all dry seasonings on and around roast, onions and peppers. Add enough cold water to rise 1-inch from covering roast. Place lid on tight.

- Bake for 7 hours if frozen, 5 hours if thawed. Remove from oven and pour beef broth over roast. Cover and let set for 15 minutes.

- To make gravy, remove roast from pan to platter. Surround with peppers and onions. Cover with foil to keep warm and moist while making gravy. Place pan on stovetop and heat drippings over medium-high heat until slow boiling.

- In small bowl combine cornstarch with equal amount of cool water. Stir well with fork. Slowly add to hot drippings and stir constantly to thicken. Add more "thickening" if needed.

TIP: Serve with mashed potatoes, your favorite vegetable and warm garlic bread.

Sirloin Pasta

1 (8 ounce) package uncooked linguine
1 (1¼ pound) boneless beef top sirloin steak
2 tablespoons olive oil, divided
2 large cloves garlic, crushed
1 (8 ounce) package portobello mushroom caps
1 medium red, yellow or green bell pepper,   ⅛-inch thick strips
2 tablespoons thinly sliced basil leaves
⅓ cup grated romano cheese

- Cook pasta according to package directions. Drain and keep warm.

- Trim fat from steak. Cut steak lengthwise in half and then crosswise into ⅛-inch thick strips.

- In large non-stick skillet, heat 1 tablespoon olive oil over medium to high heat until hot. Add beef and garlic, half at a time, and stir fry 1 to 2 minutes or until outside surface is no longer pink. Remove. Season with ½ teaspoon each of salt and pepper.

- In same skillet, heat 1 tablespoon oil until hot. Cut mushrooms in half and cut cross-wise in ¼-inch slices. Add mushrooms and bell pepper strips. Stir fry 3 to 4 minutes or until mushrooms are tender. Return beef to pan, add basil and toss. Place linguine on platter; spoon beef mixture on top. Sprinkle with cheese.

Sloppy Joes

2 pounds ground beef
½ cup barbeque sauce
1 large onion
¼ cup packed brown sugar
2 teaspoons chili powder
3 teaspoons prepared mustard

- Brown ground beef and drain. Mix remaining ingredients with ½ cup water and 1 teaspoon salt in skillet with ground meat. Heat and serve on hamburger buns.

Round Steak Pie

1 double piecrust
1 cup uncooked round steak, cut in ½-inch pieces
3 - 4 cups thinly sliced potatoes
3 slices bacon, chopped
1 tablespoon parsley flakes
1½ tablespoons butter, thinly sliced

- Preheat oven to 400°. Place unbaked bottom crust in 10-inch deep-dish pie pan. Mix steak, potatoes, bacon, parsley, 2 tablespoons water and salt and pepper to taste. Add to piecrust and top with butter slices. Cover with top crust and seal.

- Cut steam vents in top crust. Bake for 15 minutes. Lower temperature to 350° and bake about 45 minutes more. Pie is done when fork easily pierces potatoes. May serve with ketchup, salsa, gravy or plain.

Jett Family Spaghetti Sauce

1 pound ground beef
1 (14 ounce) bottle ketchup
1 (15 ounce) can tomato sauce
¾ cup sugar
1 tablespoon chili powder
1 (12 ounce) package spaghetti, cooked, drained

- Brown ground beef, season with salt and pepper and drain. Combine ketchup, tomato sauce, sugar and chili powder. Heat on medium, stirring occasionally, until boiling.

- Remove from heat and combine with ground beef. Mix sauce with cooked spaghetti. Heat and serve.

We use 40% of the average steer for beef; the entire remaining steer is used for beef by-products. Stearic acid, used to make automobile tires hold their shape, comes from cattle. The hide from one cow can make 144 baseballs, 20 footballs or 12 basketballs.

Italian-Spaghetti Pizza

1 (8 ounce) package spaghetti
1 cup milk
2 eggs
1 pound ground beef
1 medium onion, chopped
1 medium green pepper, seeded, chopped
1 (32 ounce) jar spaghetti sauce
½ teaspoon oregano
1 (4 ounce) can sliced mushrooms
1 (12 count) package sliced pepperoni
1 (8 ounce) package shredded mozzarella cheese
1 cup shredded cheddar cheese

- Preheat oven to 350°. Break spaghetti, cook according to package directions and drain. Put in sprayed 9 x 13-inch baking pan. Combine milk and beaten eggs and pour over spaghetti. Cook ground beef, onion and green pepper in skillet and drain well. Stir in spaghetti sauce and oregano. Pour over spaghetti.

- Place mushrooms and pepperoni on top. Bake for 20 minutes. Sprinkle with cheeses and bake additional 10 minutes.

Pork Chop and Rice Dinner

4 (6 ounce) lean center-cut pork chops
¼ cup chopped onion
¼ cup chopped green pepper
1 (15 ounce) can diced tomatoes
1 cup uncooked long-grain rice
½ cup fresh mushrooms, sliced
¼ teaspoon dry mustard

• Cook pork chops in non-stick skillet over medium heat. Drain and set aside. Saute onion and green pepper until tender.

• Combine tomatoes and remaining ingredients and 1 teaspoon salt and add to skillet. Place pork chops on top of mixture in skillet. Cover and simmer 30 minutes or until rice is tender.

Zucchini-Pork Casserole

4 cups sliced zucchini
1 pound ground pork, browned, drained
1½ cups cracker crumbs
3 eggs, beaten
½ cup (1 stick) butter, melted
1½ cups shredded processed cheese
1 cup milk

• Preheat oven to 350°. Mix all ingredients in baking dish and bake for 45 minutes.

Rhubarb-Pork Casserole

4 (¾-inch) thick pork loin chops, trimmed
2½ cups soft breadcrumbs, divided
½ cup packed brown sugar
¼ cup all purpose-flour
1 teaspoon ground cinnamon
3 cups (1-inch pieces) fresh or frozen rhubarb

- Preheat oven to 350°. In large, sprayed skillet, brown pork chops and season with black pepper. Remove and keep warm. Combine ¼ cup pan drippings (add water if necessary) with 1½ cups breadcrumbs. Reserve ½ cup crumbs and sprinkle crumbs into sprayed 9 x 13-inch baking.

- Combine brown sugar, flour, cinnamon and rhubarb and spoon half over crumbs. Arrange pork chops on top. Spoon remaining rhubarb mixture over chops. Cover and bake at 350° for 30 to 40 minutes.

- Uncover and sprinkle with reserved crumbs. Bake 10 to 15 minutes longer or until meat juices run clear.

Pork is the "Other White Meat" because it is low-fat and nutritious. Pork is a good source of many vitamins and minerals important to your well-balanced diet.

143

Baked Pork Chops and Apples

6 (1-inch) pork chops
1½ teaspoons sage
1 pound carrots
2 cups sliced onions
1 pound tart apples, pared, quartered
¼ cup packed brown sugar

- Preheat oven to 325°. Trim fat from pork chops. On wax paper, combine sage, 1½ teaspoons salt and ¼ teaspoon pepper. Dip both sides of chops in seasoning.

- Slice carrots and put in layer of 3-quart baking dish. Top with half of onions. Add chops, sprinkle with remaining onions. Arrange apple quarters over all and sprinkle with brown sugar.

- Bake covered for 2 hours. Remove cover and baste with pan juices. Bake for 30 minutes or until tender.

Insulin is made from pig's adrenal glands and helps people with diabetes lower their blood sugar.

Hungarian Pups
(Cabbage Rolls)

1½ pounds ground pork
1 cup uncooked rice
1 large onion, chopped
Cabbage leaves
1 (15 ounce) can diced tomatoes
1 (15 ounce) can sauerkraut

- Mix meat, rice, onion, salt and pepper to taste in bowl and set aside. Separate cabbage leaves and pour boiling water over each to wilt. Form small "pups" of meat mixture and wrap in cabbage leaf. Lay in large soup pot.

- Pour tomatoes and sauerkraut over pups. Add enough water to barely cover. Cook over low heat for 1½ hours. May add salt and pepper to taste.

- Makes 8 large "pups." Yields: 4 to 6 servings.

Illinois currently ranks fourth in the U.S. in pork production. There are 4,600 hog farms in Illinois. In 2003, Illinois produced 1.83 billion pounds of pork. The pork industry in Illinois employees 18,500 people.

Herb-Rubbed Roast Pork

1 tablespoon sugar
2 teaspoons ground sage
2 teaspoons dried sweet marjoram, crushed
1 teaspoon dry mustard
1 teaspoon celery seed
5 pounds pork loin roast

- Preheat oven to 325°. In small bowl, combine all seasonings with 1 teaspoon salt and ½ teaspoon pepper. Thoroughly rub roast with mixture. Cover with plastic wrap and let stand at least 4 hours or overnight in refrigerator.

- Set meat on rack in shallow roasting pan. Insert meat thermometer. Roast uncovered for 2½ to 3 hours or until thermometer registers 170°. Loosely cover and let rest for 15 minutes before carving. Garnish with fresh herbs. Yields: 8 servings.

Hogs provide us with more products than any other animal. A pig will eat about 870 pounds of corn and 120 pounds of protein to reach its market weight. Pigs will weigh about 250 pounds when they go to market.

Pork Pockets

Bacon (2 strips per pocket)
Pork tenderloin, cut into 1½-inch medallions
Sweet onion, thinly sliced
1 tomato, sliced
Portobello mushrooms, sliced
Provolone cheese slices

- Lay 2 slices bacon, criss-crossed, on flat surface. Place 1 pork medallion in center of bacon. Add salt and pepper. Place 1 slice onion, tomato and portobello mushrooms on top of pork.

- Wrap bacon up and around all. Secure with toothpick. Heat grill to medium. Place pockets on grill, close lid and cook for 40 to 45 minutes. Place 1 piece provolone on each pocket and cook 5 minutes more.

TIP: Pork, onion, tomato and mushroom wrapped in bacon can be made ahead of time.

Pig heart valves have been used to replace damaged human heart valves.

147

Sweet-and-Sour Pork

1½ pounds lean pork, cubed
1 (20 ounce) can pineapple tidbits with juice
¼ cup packed brown sugar
2 tablespoons cornstarch
¼ cup vinegar
1 tablespoon soy sauce
¾ cup green bell pepper strips
¼ cup thinly sliced onions
4 cups cooked rice

- Brown pork slowly in small amount of oil in skillet and set aside. Drain pineapple and save juice. Combine brown sugar, ¼ cup water and cornstarch in saucepan. Add pineapple juice, vinegar and soy sauce. Cook and stir over low heat until thick.

- Pour over hot cooked pork and let stand 10 minutes. Add pineapple, green bell pepper and onion. Cook 5 minutes longer. Serve over cooked rice.

A sow gives birth to a litter of piglets twice a year! A litter is a bunch of piglets born at the same time. The average litter has eight to twelve piglets Pigs are pregnant for three months, three weeks, and three days! Farrowing in hog production means giving birth.

Pork Tenderloin with Blackberry Sauce

2 (1 pound) pork tenderloins
1 teaspoon coarsely ground whole allspice
¼ cup (½ stick) butter, divided
½ cup diced shallots
⅔ cup dry white wine
3 tablespoons seedless, blackberry fruit spread

- Sprinkle pork evenly with 1 teaspoon each of salt and black pepper and allspice. Cover and chill 30 minutes. Grill pork over medium to high heat (350° to 400°) for 20 minutes or until meat thermometer inserted into thickest portion registers 160°, turn pork once.

- Remove from grill and let stand for 10 minutes. Melt 2 tablespoons butter in small saucepan over medium to high heat. Add shallots and saute 5 minutes or until tender. Add wine. Cook 13 minutes or until liquid reduces by half. Reduce heat to low. Whisk in fruit spread and remaining butter. Cook 2 minutes or until it thickens slightly. Cut pork into ¼-inch slices. Drizzle blackberry sauce over pork.

A female pig is called a sow. A boar is a male pig. A barrow is a male pig that is not used for breeding. Swine is a broad term for pigs.

Honey-Barbecued Pork Loin

½ cup honey
½ cup ketchup
½ cup chili sauce
¼ cup finely chopped green pepper
¼ cup finely chopped onion
2 tablespoons cider vinegar
1 tablespoon prepared mustard
1 tablespoon Worcestershire sauce
2 drops hot sauce
2 - 3 pound boneless pork loin roast

- Combine honey, ketchup, chili sauce, green pepper, onion, vinegar, mustard, Worcestershire and hot sauce in 2-quart saucepan. Cook over high heat until mixture comes to a boil. Reduce heat to low. Simmer 30 minutes. Pour sauce into glass bowl. Cover and refrigerate.

- Preheat oven to 350°. Season loin with salt and pepper in shallow roasting pan. Spoon half glaze over pork. Bake and baste with remaining glaze every 15 minutes until meat thermometer inserted in center of roast reads 145° to 150°. This takes approximately 2 hours 15 minutes. Yields: 12 to 16 servings.

Pigs are very smart. They rank as the fourth most intelligent animal.

Hearty Ham with Raisin Sauce

**1 (14 pound) fully cooked, semi-boneless, sugar-
  cured ham**
20 - 25 whole cloves
1 cup raisins
1½ cups firmly packed light brown sugar
2 teaspoons soy sauce
¼ teaspoon ground cloves
1 (20 ounce) can crushed pineapple in heavy syrup

- Preheat oven to 325°. Trim fat from ham and score surface in diamond pattern and stud with whole cloves. Place ham in large roasting pan and tent with foil.

- Bake 3½ hours or about 15 minutes per pound. Drain pan drippings into blender. Add raisins, brown sugar, soy sauce and ground cloves. Process until pureed.

- Pour mixture into medium saucepan. Stir in undrained pineapple. Simmer, stirring occasionally, for 15 minutes. Brush ham with pineapple mixture.

- Continue baking ham, basting with pineapple mixture every 10 minutes, for 1 hour. Remove ham to serving platter. Cool for 15 to 25 minutes before carving. Garnish with kale and fresh pineapple (optional). Yields: 12 to 16 servings.

Ham Balls in Brown Sauce

1½ pounds ground ham
1 pound ground beef
2 cups breadcrumbs
2 eggs, well beaten
1 cup milk

Sauce:
1 cup packed brown sugar
1 teaspoon dry mustard
½ cup vinegar

- Mix all ham ingredients and form into balls and place in sprayed baking pan. Mix sauce ingredients and pour over ham balls. Baste frequently. Bake at 325° for 1 hour.

Ham and Rice Casserole

4 cups cooked, cubed ham
2 cups cooked rice
1 cup shredded cheddar cheese
1 cup chopped onion
2 tablespoons butter
¼ cup flour
1½ teaspoons dill weed
3 cups milk
Italian seasoned breadcrumbs

- Preheat oven to 350°. Combine ham, rice, and cheese in 2-quart baking dish. In skillet, cook onion in butter until tender. Stir in flour and dill weed; add milk. Cook and stir until bubbly. Pour over ham mixture and stir. Cover with Italian breadcrumbs. Bake, uncovered, at 350° for 25 minutes.

Ham-Asparagus Pasta Delight

1 medium onion, diced
3 carrots, thinly sliced
5½ cups cut fresh asparagus
¼ cup butter
¼ heaping cup flour
2 cups milk, divided
1 (8 ounce) package cubed processed cheese
1 pound ham, cooked, cut up
8 ounces angel hair pasta, cooked

- Preheat oven to 350°. In large saucepan over medium-high heat cook onion, carrots and asparagus in about ½ cup water for 10 minutes or until carrots are tender. Transfer to large bowl.

- In same saucepan on medium heat, melt butter and add flour, stirring until mixed well. Stir in milk and cheese and stir constantly until mixture thickens and is smooth. Add ham, vegetables, pasta and salt and pepper to taste. Spoon into greased 3-quart baking pan; cover and bake 25 minutes.

TIP: 5 ½ cups fresh asparagus = about 1½ pounds

A pig's squeal ranges from 110-115 decibels; the noise from a Concorde jet is recorded at 112 decibels!

153

Sausage and Wild Rice

1 (6 ounce) box long-grain wild rice
1 pound sausage
1 (4 ounce) small can mushrooms
1 (8 ounce) carton sour cream

- Prepare rice according to package directions. Brown sausage and drain. Mix all ingredients, warm and serve.

All-In-One Sausage Skillet

6 slices bacon
1 medium head cabbage, cut in wedges
1 medium onion, chopped
2 tablespoons sugar
1 teaspoon minced garlic
1 pound kielbasa sausage, sliced

- Fry bacon until crisp. Remove and drain. Set aside. Add cabbage wedges, onion, sugar, ¼ cup water, garlic and 1 teaspoon salt to bacon drippings. Cook, covered, over medium heat for 10 to 15 minutes and stir several times. Add kielbasa. Return cover and continue to cook for 10 to 15 minutes or until sausage heats. Crumbled bacon, sprinkle on top and serve.

Finger Lickin' Good Barbecued Short Ribs

3 - 3½ pounds short ribs
1 cup ketchup
1 medium onion, chopped
¼ cup packed brown sugar
3 tablespoons Worcestershire sauce
2 teaspoons garlic salt
2 teaspoons prepared mustard
1 lemon, sliced

- Preheat oven to 350°. Cut ribs into serving-size pieces and place in baking dish. Combine remaining ingredients with ½ cup water; pour over ribs. Cover and bake for 1½ to 2 hours until tender. Skim off fat and serve with sauce.

Italian Casserole

4 pounds chuck roast, deer or elk roast
Garlic powder
Oregano, crushed
2 onions, sliced
1 (12 ounce) jar pepperoncini peppers with liquid
1 (14 ounce) can beef broth
1 (12 ounce) can beer

- Preheat oven to 300°. Place roast in 9 x 13-inch baking pan. Sprinkle both sides of meat with salt, pepper, garlic powder and oregano. Lay onion slices and pepperoncini peppers on top. Pour broth, pepper juices (sparingly) and beer on top; cover with foil. Bake for 4 hours.

Easy Pasta Casserole (Venison)

1 (7 ounce) package elbow macaroni
1 pound venison ground meat
¼ pound ground pork sausage
1 (10 ounce) can cream of mushroom soup
½ teaspoon dry mustard
½ cup evaporated milk
½ teaspoon thyme
1 tablespoon Worcestershire sauce
½ cup shredded cheddar cheese

- Preheat oven to 350°. Cook macaroni according to package directions and drain. In skillet, with a little oil brown and crumble ground venison and sausage. Stir in macaroni, soup, mustard, milk, thyme, Worcestershire and salt and pepper to taste. Spoon into greased 3-quart baking dish; cover and bake 30 minutes.

- Remove from oven and sprinkle cheese over top and return to oven for 5 minutes.

Most pigs are raised indoors in stalls to keep them safe from extreme weather conditions. Pigs can't sweat, so farmers use sprinklers and fans to keep them cool.

Three-Cheese Enchiladas

1½ cups shredded Monterey Jack cheese, divided
1½ cups shredded cheddar cheese, divided
1 (3 ounce) package cream cheese, softened
1 cup salsa, divided
1 medium green bell pepper, diced
½ cup sliced green onion
1 teaspoon cumin
8 flour tortillas
Shredded lettuce
Chopped tomato
Sliced black olives

- Combine 1 cup Monterey Jack cheese, 1 cup cheddar cheese, cream cheese, ¼ cup salsa, green bell pepper, onions and cumin. Mix well.

- Spoon ¼ cup cheese mixture into each tortilla. Roll and place seam-side down in greased 9 x 13-inch baking dish.

- Spoon remaining salsa evenly over enchiladas and cover with remaining cheeses. Bake at 350° for 20 to 25 minutes or until hot. Top with lettuce, tomato and black olives. Serve with additional salsa, if desired. Yields: 4 servings.

Super Spinach Lasagna

9 lasagna noodles
¾ cup chopped onion
1 - 2 cloves garlic, minced
2 tablespoons butter
1 (16 ounce) package frozen chopped spinach
1 (8 ounce) package shredded mozzarella cheese
¾ cup sour cream
1 egg
¼ cup (½ stick) butter
¼ cup flour
1½ teaspoons chicken bouillon
2 cups milk
½ cup shredded parmesan cheese

- Cook noodles according to package directions and set aside. Saute onion and garlic in butter for 5 minutes. Add spinach, mozzarella cheese, sour cream and egg. Heat on medium heat until mixture melts and mixes.

- In another pan make white sauce with butter, flour, bouillon, ½ teaspoon salt and ⅛ teaspoon pepper. Stir in milk. Bring to boil and stir constantly. Boil for 1 minute. Layer mixture 3 times, first with spinach mixture, noodles and white sauce. Sprinkle with parmesan cheese. Bake at 350° for 30 to 35 minutes, or until hot and bubbly.

PUTTIN' ON THE FEEDBAG

Cakes and Pies
Cookies and Bars
Desserts and Candy

Candy Bar Cake

1 (18 ounce) box chocolate cake mix
1 (8 ounce) package cream cheese, softened
1 cup powdered sugar
½ cup sugar
1 (12 ounce) carton whipped topping, thawed
8 (1.5 ounce) chocolate bars, chopped
1 (5 ounce) chocolate bar

- Preheat oven to 350°. Prepare cake batter according to package directions. Pour batter into sprayed 3 (8-inch) round baking pans. Bake for 20 to 25 minutes and cool in pans for 10 minutes. Remove from pans and cool completely.

- Combine cream cheese, powdered sugar and sugar. Beat on medium speed until mixture is creamy. Stir in whipped topping and chopped chocolate bars. Spread icing between cake layers and on top of cake. Use carrot peeler to slice thin layer from large chocolate bar. As you slice, chocolate will curl. (This is easier if chocolate is slightly soft.) Put curls on top of cake for decoration. Keep refrigerated.

Soybeans can be found in many of your favorite chocolate candy bars.

160

Chocolate-Pistachio Cake

1 (18 ounce) package yellow cake mix
1 (6 ounce) package pistachio instant pudding
½ cup orange juice
4 eggs
½ cup oil
¾ cup chocolate syrup

- Preheat oven to 350°. In large bowl, combine cake mix, pudding mix, orange juice, ½ cup water, eggs and oil. Beat on medium speed for 2 minutes. Pour about ¾ batter into well greased, floured 12-cup cake pan. Add syrup to remaining batter in bowl, mix well and pour over batter in pan. Bake for 1 hour. Cool for 10 minutes and remove from pan and cool on wire rack.

TIP: For an extra special touch, you can sprinkle confectioners sugar on top of this gorgeous cake.

In the 1920's, Dr. John Harvey Kellogg developed soy milk and meat substitutes from soybeans.

Fabulously Fresh Apple Cake

1 cup vegetable oil
2 cups sugar
2 eggs, well beaten
1 teaspoon baking soda
2 cups flour
1 teaspoon cinnamon
1 cup chopped nuts
2 cups peeled, chopped apples

- Preheat oven to 300°. In medium bowl, mix all ingredients plus 1 teaspoon salt. Spread into sprayed jelly-roll pan. Bake at 300° for 1 hour. When toothpick inserted in center of cake comes out clean, cake is done.

Brown Sugar Icing:
3 tablespoons cornstarch
½ cup packed brown sugar
½ cup sugar
1 teaspoon vanilla
½ cup (1 stick) butter

- In small saucepan, combine cornstarch, both sugars, plus ½ cup water and cook, stirring constantly until thick; add vanilla, butter and a little salt and mix until butter has melted. Drizzle over cake and sides.

Dump Cake

1 (20 ounce) can cherry pie filling
1 (8 ounce) can crushed pineapple with juice
1 (18 ounce) box yellow cake mix
½ cup chopped nuts
½ cup (1 stick) butter, sliced
Whipped topping

- Preheat oven to 350°. In 9 x 13-inch sprayed pan layer pie filling and pineapple. Sprinkle dry cake mix on top. Sprinkle nuts over mixture and dot with butter. Bake for 35 minutes. Serve with whipped topping.

Luscious Lemon Cooler Cream Cake

1 (18 ounce) box lemon cake mix
2 (3 ounce) boxes lemon gelatin, divided
1 cup milk
1 (3 ounce) package instant vanilla pudding mix
1 (8 ounce) carton whipped topping

- Prepare cake according to package directions and bake in greased and floured 9 x 13-inch baking pan. Poke holes on cake's top with fork. In medium bowl, combine 1 box gelatin mix with 1 cup hot water and 1 cup cold water. Stir mixture until gelatin dissolves, and pour over cake. Chill in refrigerator until cool.

- In large bowl, stir together milk, pudding mix and remaining box gelatin until powders dissolve. Fold in whipped topping and spread mixture over cake. Refrigerate.

Mandarin Orange Layer Cake

1 (18 ounce) box white cake mix
2 eggs
⅓ cup sweetened applesauce
1 (11 ounce) can mandarin oranges with juice
1 (8 ounce) carton frozen whipped topping, thawed
1 (8 ounce) and crushed pineapple with juice
1 (3 ounce) package instant vanilla pudding mix

- Preheat oven to 325°. In medium bowl, combine cake mix, eggs, applesauce and oranges. Beat on low for 30 seconds and beat on medium for 2 minutes.

- Spray 2 (9-inch) cake pans and line with parchment paper. Pour batter into pans and bake for 30 minutes or until toothpick inserted in center comes out clean. Cool in pan for 10 minutes. Move to wire rack and cool completely.

- In another mixing bowl, beat together whipped topping, pineapple and pudding mix. Spread frosting on first layer and place second layer on top. Spread remaining frosting on top and sides of cake. Refrigerate.

Half of all apples grown in the U.S. are made into apple juice, applesauce, or dehydrated apple products.

Moon Cake

½ cup (1 stick) butter
1 cup flour
4 eggs
2 (3 ounce) packages instant pudding (any flavor)
3 cups milk
1 (8 ounce) package cream cheese, softened
1 (8 ounce) carton whipped topping
Chocolate syrup or sauce
Chopped nuts

- Preheat oven to 400°. Bring butter and 1 cup water to boil.
  Add flour and stir well over heat until batter turns into a
  ball. Remove from heat and cool slightly. Add eggs, one at
  a time and beat well after each addition.

- Spread mixture onto 10 x 15-inch cookie sheet and bake for
  25 minutes. Crust will look like moon's surface, thus the
  title "Moon Cake."

- Mix pudding and milk according to package directions.
  Beat in cream cheese and blend well. Spread on cooled
  crust and chill for 20 minutes.

- Top with whipped topping, drizzle with chocolate syrup
  and sprinkle with chopped nuts.

Peanut Butter Sheet Cake

2 cups flour
2 cups sugar
1 teaspoon baking soda
½ cup oil
¾ cup (1½ sticks) butter
½ cup peanut butter
2 eggs, beaten
½ cup buttermilk
1 teaspoon vanilla

- Preheat oven to 350°. Combine flour, sugar, baking soda and ½ teaspoon salt. In saucepan bring oil, butter, peanut butter and 1 cup water to a boil. Mix into dry ingredients. Add eggs, buttermilk and vanilla and blend well. Pour batter into greased 11 x 15 x 1-inch sheet baking pan. Bake for 15 to 18 minutes in 350°.

Icing:
½ cup evaporated milk
1 cup sugar
1 tablespoon butter
½ cup crunchy peanut butter
½ cup miniature marshmallows
1 teaspoon vanilla

- While cake bakes, combine milk, sugar and butter in saucepan and cook for 2 minutes. Remove from heat, add peanut butter and marshmallows and stir until they melt. Stir in vanilla. Pour over warm cake and spread to cover.

Pineapple Sheet Cake

2 cups sugar
1 teaspoon baking soda
2 cups flour
½ cup oil
2 eggs
1 (20 ounce) can crushed pineapple with juice
1 teaspoon vanilla

- Preheat oven to 350°. Mix dry ingredients in bowl, add oil, eggs, pineapple and vanilla and mix thoroughly. Bake in sprayed 9 x 13-inch cake pan for 35 minutes.

Icing:
1 (8 ounce) cream cheese, softened
½ cup (1 stick butter), softened
1 teaspoon vanilla
1¾ cups powdered sugar

- Beat together cream cheese and butter until creamy. Add vanilla and powdered sugar. Beat until smooth and spread on cooled cake.

TIP: Sprinkle pecans or nuts on top for an added special touch.

Sweet Cinnamon-Rhubarb Cake

½ cup shortening
1 cup packed brown sugar
1 cup sugar, divided
1 egg
1 teaspoon vanilla
2 cups flour
1 teaspoon baking soda
1 cup buttermilk*
2 cups frozen chopped rhubarb, thawed
1 teaspoon cinnamon

- Preheat oven to 350°. In medium bowl, cream shortening, brown sugar, ½ cup sugar until fluffy.
Add egg and vanilla and beat 2 minutes.

- Combine dry ingredients plus ½ teaspoon salt and add to creamed mixture a little at a time, alternating with buttermilk. Beat well after each addition. Stir in rhubarb. Pour into 9 x 13-inch sprayed floured pan. Combine remaining sugar and cinnamon and sprinkle over batter. Bake for 40 to 45 minutes.

*TIP: To make buttermilk, mix 1 cup milk with 1 tablespoon lemon juice or vinegar and let milk rest about 10 minutes.

Really Special Red Velvet Cake

2 ounces red food coloring
3 tablespoons cocoa
½ cup shortening
1½ cups sugar
2 eggs
1 teaspoon vanilla
2¼ cups flour
1 cup buttermilk
1 tablespoon vinegar
1 teaspoon baking soda

- Preheat oven to 350°. Mix food coloring and cocoa and set aside. Cream shortening and sugar. Add eggs and mix well. Stir in food coloring-cocoa mixture and vanilla. Add flour mixed with ½ teaspoon salt a little at a time alternating with buttermilk and mix well. Stir in vinegar and baking soda.

- Pour mixture into 3 (8-inch) cake pans lined with wax paper. Bake for 20 minutes or until toothpick inserted in center comes out clean.

Elizabeth's Cake Icing

½ cup shortening
½ cup (1 stick) butter, softened
1 (1 pound) box powdered sugar
1 teaspoon vanilla

- Cream shortening and butter. Add sugar, vanilla and 2 tablespoons water and beat until creamy. Spread evenly over cake.

169

Very Best Chocolate Cake

2 cups sugar
1¾ cups flour
¾ cup cocoa
1½ teaspoons baking powder
1½ teaspoons baking soda
2 eggs
1 cup milk
½ cup vegetable oil
2 teaspoons vanilla extract

Frosting:
½ cup (1 stick) butter
⅔ cup cocoa
2 cups powdered sugar
½ cup milk
1 teaspoon vanilla extract

- Preheat oven to 350°. In large bowl, stir together sugar, flour, cocoa, baking powder, baking soda and   1 teaspoon salt. Add eggs, milk, oil and vanilla and beat on medium speed for 2 minutes. Stir in 1 cup boiling water. (batter will be thin).

- Pour batter into 2 sprayed, round 9-inch cake pans and bake for 30 to 35 minutes or until toothpick inserted in center comes out clean.

- Melt butter in microwave and stir in cocoa. Add powdered sugar and milk alternately and blend well after each addition until mixture reaches frosting consistency. Add vanilla. Add a little more milk, if needed, to make spreading consistency.

Hello-Jello Cake

1 (18 ounce) box cake mix
¾ cup strawberry soda
1 (3 ounce) box strawberry gelatin
1 (3 ounce) package instant vanilla pudding mix
1½ cups milk
1 (8 ounce) carton whipped topping

- Prepare cake mix according to package directions and bake in greased and floured
9 x 13-inch baking dish; cool completely.

- Poke holes in cake with fork. In small bowl, mix strawberry soda, strawberry gelatin and ¾ cup water and pour over cake. In small bowl, mix pudding and milk and fold in whipped topping. Spread pudding mixture over cake. Refrigerate cake.

Awesome Angel Food Cake

2 cups egg whites at room temperature
2 teaspoons cream of tartar
2 teaspoons vanilla
1¼ cups sugar
1½ cups cake flour, sifted

- Preheat oven to 350°. Beat egg whites, cream of tarter, ½ teaspoon salt and vanilla until frothy. Gradually add 1¼ cups sugar and beat until stiff. Fold in flour. Spoon into 10-inch tube pan. Bake for 1 hour or until toothpick inserted in center comes out clean.

Hot Milk Sponge Cake

2 eggs
1 cup sugar
1 cup sifted cake flour (1 cup regular flour less 2 tablespoons)
1 teaspoon baking powder
½ cup boiling milk
1 tablespoon butter
1 teaspoon vanilla

- Preheat oven at 350°. In large bowl, beat eggs and slowly add sugar. Beat until thick and lemon-colored; add flour, ½ teaspoon salt and baking powder and mix well. Add boiling milk, in which butter has been melted and vanilla and beat well.

- Pour mixture into sprayed 9 x 9-inch baking pan and bake 25 to 30 minutes or until brown.

TIP: This is an excellent cake for making peanut squares or for splitting and adding a pudding-type filling of your choice.

Many foods in your kitchen contain soy, mayonnaise and salad dressing to name a few.

Unbelievable Lemon Cheesecake

2 (3 ounce) boxes lemon gelatin
2 tablespoons lemon juice
1 (8 ounce) package cream cheese, softened
½ cup sugar
1 teaspoon vanilla
1 (12 ounce) can evaporated milk, chilled, whipped
3 cups graham cracker crumbs
½ cup (1 stick) butter, melted

- Preheat oven to 325°. Dissolve gelatin in 2 cups boiling water. Add lemon juice. and chill. Mixture will thicken slightly.

- In medium bowl, beat together cream cheese, sugar and vanilla, add gelatin and blend well. Fold in stiffly whipped evaporated milk. In medium bowl, combine graham cracker crumbs and butter. Pack two-thirds of graham cracker mixture on bottom of 9 x 13-inch baking pan.

- Bake for 10 minutes, cool, add filling and sprinkle remaining crumbs on top. Refrigerate.

Crayons made from soybeans have better color, cost less to make, and don't rub off like other crayons.

Praline Cheesecake

¼ cup (½ stick) butter, melted
1 cup graham cracker crumbs
1 cup finely chopped pecans, divided
½ cup packed brown sugar
1 cup milk chocolate-toffee bits, divided
1 cup sugar
4 (8 ounce) packages cream cheese, softened
4 large eggs

- Preheat oven to 300°. Stir butter, crumbs, ½ cup pecans and brown sugar in medium bowl. Press crumb mixture evenly into bottom and sides of sprayed 10-inch springform pan. Bake for 10 to 12 minutes or until edges brown lightly. Remove from oven and immediately sprinkle ½ cup toffee bits on hot, partially baked crumbs.

- Combine sugar and cream cheese in large bowl and beat mixture on medium speed, scraping bowl occasionally, until creamy. Add eggs 1 at a time and beat until they mix well. Do not overbeat. Pour over crust. Bake for 65 to 70 minutes or until edges set and is brown lightly.

- Loosen cheesecake from pan by running sprayed knife around inside edge of pan. Sprinkle remaining toffee bits and remaining chopped pecans on top. Cool 1 hour on cooling rack and chill, uncovered, for 1 hour. Cover and keep refrigerated.

Heavenly Cheesecake

Crust:
1 cup sugar
3 egg whites
½ teaspoon cream of tartar
1 teaspoon vanilla
1 sleeve round buttery crackers

• Preheat oven to 350°. In medium bowl, whisk all ingredients except crackers, by hand. Gently crush crackers while still in sleeve. Add crackers to egg mixture, mix well and press into 8-inch, round pie pan. Bake for 20 minutes and set aside to cool.

Filling:
1 (8 ounce) package cream cheese, softened
1 cup powdered sugar
4 tablespoons milk
1 (8 ounce) carton whipped topping
1 (20 ounce) can cherry pie filling

• Combine cream cheese, powdered sugar and milk and beat until smooth. Fold in whipped topping and pour into cooled crust; refrigerate. Top with pie filling before serving.

TIP: This cheesecake is truly heavenly, no matter what flavor filling you top it off with. Try another favorite.

Peanut Butter Cheesecake Minis

Crust:
1½ cups graham cracker crumbs
4 tablespoons sugar
¼ cup (½ stick) butter, melted
12 bite-size peanut butter cups

Filling:
2 (8 ounce) packages cream cheese, softened
1 cup sugar
¼ cup flour
1 teaspoon vanilla or almond extract
2 eggs

- Preheat oven to 350°. Place paper cupcake liner in each cup of muffin pan. Mix graham cracker crumbs, sugar and butter in bowl until crumbs are moist. Press crust into bottom of each muffin cup and place 1 peanut butter cup into center.

- Beat cream cheese with mixer until fluffy, add sugar, flour and vanilla and beat well. Add eggs one at a time and beat well after each addition. Spoon cream cheese mixture over peanut butter cups. Bake for about 20 minutes or just until set. Allow to cool completely before serving.

Chocolate Chip Cheesecake

2 (8 ounce) packages cream cheese, softened
½ cup sugar
½ teaspoon vanilla
2 eggs
¾ cup miniature semi-sweet chocolate chips, divided
1 (9 ounce) prepared graham cracker piecrust

- Preheat oven to 350°. In bowl, blend cream cheese, sugar and vanilla at medium speed until mixture blends well.

- Add eggs and mix until they blend; stir in ½ cup chocolate chips. Pour into crust and sprinkle remaining chocolate chips on top. Bake for 40 minutes.

Soybean oil, a renewable resource, is used to make soy ink. More than 80,000 newspapers in the United States use soy inks.

Speed Pie-Baking Hints

Here's a fast way to bake pies

- Cook fruit pies with double crusts for 8 minutes on HIGH in microwave. Bake at 400° for 15 minutes on bottom rack of oven.

- Cook pecan pie for 8 minutes on HIGH in microwave. Bake at 375° for 15 minutes on bottom rack of oven.

- Cook pumpkin pie for 8 minutes on HIGH in microwave. Bake at 375° for 20 minutes on bottom rack of oven.

- Cook soft pie filling in microwave on HIGH until thick.

Rosie's Apple Pie

1 teaspoon lemon juice, stirred into apples
4 - 5 cups apples (Jonathon Gold is good)
1½ cups sugar
2 tablespoons flour
Dash salt
1 teaspoon apple pie spice
1 teaspoon butter, on top of apples
2 (9-inch) piecrusts

- Squeeze 1 to 2 teaspoons lemon juice over apples. Mix all ingredients and pour into piecrusts. Top with crust or lattice cut from piecrust top. Cook in microwave for 8 minutes on HIGH and then cook15 minutes at 400° on bottom rack of oven.

178

Almond-Macaroon Cherry Pie

1 (9-inch) pie shell, unbaked
1 (20 ounce) can cherry pie filling
½ teaspoon cinnamon
1 teaspoon lemon juice

Topping:
1 cup shredded coconut
½ cup sliced almonds
¼ cup sugar
¼ cup milk
1 teaspoon butter, melted
¼ teaspoon almond extract
1 egg, beaten

- Preheat oven to 350°. Roll out pastry and place in 9-inch pie pan. In large bowl, combine pie filling, cinnamon and lemon juice, mix lightly and pour into pie pan. Bake for 20 minutes.

- Combine all topping ingredients in medium bowl and mix until they blend. Remove pie from oven after 20 minutes, spread topping evenly over cherries and return to oven. Bake additional 15 to 30 minutes or until crust and topping are golden brown.

Old-Fashioned Country Coconut Pie

1¾ cups milk, divided
2 (3 ounce) boxes instant coconut pudding
1 teaspoon vanilla
1 (8 ounce) carton whipped topping
1 (6 ounce) piecrust, baked

- Beat together milk and pudding mix, mixing until creamy. Fold in whipped topping and vanilla. Pour into piecrust. Chill.

Cranberry-Raspberry Pie

2 (9-inch) double piecrusts
1 (12 ounce) package frozen red raspberries with juice, thawed
¼ cup quick-cooking tapioca
1 (12 ounce) package fresh or frozen cranberries, coarsely chopped
2¼ cups sugar, divided
½ teaspoon almond extract
1 tablespoon milk

- Preheat oven to 375°. Put 1 piecrust on bottom of pie plate. In large bowl, combine raspberries with juice and tapioca; add cranberries, 2 cups sugar and almond extract. Stir well and let stand for 15 minutes. Pour fruit into piecrust and add top crust. Brush top crust with milk and sprinkle with remaining sugar. Cover edges with foil. Bake for 30 minutes. Remove foil and bake for 20 to 30 minutes until top is golden and juice is clear. Serve with ice cream or sweetened whipped cream. Makes 1 (9-inch) pie.

Delectable Cream Pie

3 cups milk
1 cup white sugar
⅓ cup cornstarch
4 egg yolks
1 teaspoon vanilla
1 (9-inch) pie shell, baked

- Mix together milk, sugar, cornstarch and egg yolks and cook in microwave on HIGH until thick, about 7 to 9 minutes. Add vanilla and pour in piecrust. Use egg whites for meringue.

TIP: Add ⅔ to 1 cup shredded coconut to filling to make coconut pie. Sprinkle coconut on meringue before baking.

Mile-High Meringue for Cream Pie:
4 egg whites
1 teaspoon cream of tartar
½ cup sugar

- Beat whites and pinch of salt until frothy. Add cream of tartar. Beat until peaks form. Add sugar slowly and heat well. Spoon on top of hot filling. Bake at 375° for 8 to 10 minutes until nicely brown.

The soybean is called the "miracle crop" because it's so high protein and vitamins.

Key Lime Pie

4 egg yolks, beaten
2 (14 ounces) cans sweetened condensed milk
1 cup key lime juice
1 (9-inch) prepared piecrust
Whipped cream

- Preheat oven to 375°. Combine egg yolks, milk and key lime juice and mix. Pour into unbaked shortbread crust and bake for 15 minutes; chill. Top with dollops of whipped cream and lime slices.

TIP: Key Lime Pie is yellow, not green. The egg yolks create the color.

Party Custard Pie

2½ cups milk
½ cup white sugar
4 eggs, beaten
1 teaspoon vanilla extract
1 teaspoon almond extract
1 (9-inch) piecrust, unbaked

- Heat milk almost to boiling and add ½ teaspoon salt and sugar. Slowly add beaten eggs and stir as you add eggs. Add flavor extracts and pour into piecrust. Bake at 400° for 20 minutes on bottom rack of oven.

Peanut Butter Pie

2 cups powdered sugar
1 (8 ounce) package cream cheese, softened
1¼ cups peanut butter
1 cup milk
1 (16 ounce) carton whipped topping
3 (6 ounce) graham cracker piecrusts
Chocolate syrup
Chopped nuts

- Cream together powdered sugar, cream cheese and peanut butter. Add milk and stir until it blends. Fold in whipped topping, pour into crusts and freeze. Before serving, top with chocolate syrup and nuts.

Butterfinger Pie

1 (8 ounce) package cream cheese, softened
1 (8 ounce) carton whipped topping
6 Butterfinger candy bars, crushed
1 (6 ounce) graham cracker piecrust

- Beat together cream cheese and whipped topping. Mix in most of candy bars, but save a few pieces to sprinkle on top. Pour cream cheese mixture into crust. Sprinkle remaining candy pieces on top. Refrigerate for 2 hours.

183

Perfect Peach Pie

2 (9-inch) piecrusts
5 cups sliced, peeled fresh peaches
1 tablespoon lemon juice
½ teaspoon almond extract
1 cup sugar
¼ cup quick-cooking tapioca
2 tablespoons butter

- Line 9-inch pie plate with bottom crust. Trim pastry to 1-inch beyond edge of pie plate and set aside.

- In bowl, combine peaches, lemon juice and almond extract. Add sugar, tapioca and ¼ teaspoon salt and toss gently. Pour into crust and dot with butter.

- Roll out remaining pastry and cut form lattice crust. Seal and flute edges. Cover edges loosely with foil and bake at 425° for 20 minutes.

- Remove foil and bake 20 for 30 minutes longer or until crust is golden brown and filling bubbles. Cool on wire rack. Yields: 6 to 8 servings.

Double-Crusted Lemon Tart

1 (15 ounce) package refrigerated all-ready piecrust
1 (20 ounce) can lemon pie filling
1 egg white, beaten, divided
½ cup powdered sugar
2 teaspoons milk

- Preheat oven to 400°. Unfold pastry dough for 1 crust and place on 12-inch pizza pan or cookie sheet. Spoon lemon filling onto dough and spread to within ¾-inch of edge. Brush edge with beaten egg white. Unfold and top with remaining pastry. Press around edge with finger to seal. Prick top surface with fork and brush with egg white.

- Bake for 20 to 25 minutes or until light brown. Cool. Stir sugar and milk together with fork until smooth and drizzle on top. Yields 10 to 12 servings. Cut with pizza cutter into pie wedges. For smaller portions cut into squares.

TIP: Cherry, apple or peach pie filling may be substituted for lemon, but it needs to bake 5 to 10 minutes longer depending on your oven.

Many countries use soybeans as a protein source rather than meat, eggs, or cheese. China uses more American soybeans than any other country. Chinese farmers were growing soybeans 5,000 years ago.

185

Strawberry-Yogurt Pie

2 (8 ounce) cartons strawberry yogurt
½ cup crushed strawberries
1 (8 ounce) carton whipped topping
1 (6 ounce) graham cracker piecrust

- Combine yogurt and fruit and fold in whipped topping. Put in piecrust and freeze for 4 hours. Refrigerate 30 minutes before serving.

Rhubarb Cobbler

6 cups rhubarb, chopped
1½ cups sugar
1 (6 ounce) box strawberry gelatin
1 (18 ounce) box white cake mix
¾ cup (1½ sticks) butter, melted

- Preheat oven to 350°. In 9 x 13-inch glass baking dish, layer in this order, rhubarb, sugar, gelatin, cake mix, 1½ cups hot water and butter. Bake for 50 to 55 minutes.

TIP: Have fun and use any of your favorite fruits in this cobbler.

Never-Fail Piecrust

1 egg
1 tablespoon sugar
2½ cups flour
1 cup shortening

- Put egg in measuring cup and beat with fork. Add water to equal ¾ cup water, add sugar and stir. Mix flour, pinch of salt and shortening until crumbly. Pour egg mixture into flour and mix. Makes 3 crusts.

Never-Fail Meringue

1 tablespoon cornstarch
3 egg whites
6 tablespoons sugar
1 teaspoon vanilla

- Blend cornstarch and 2 tablespoons cold water in saucepan. Add ½ cup boiling water and cook until clear and thick. Let stand until cool. Beat egg whites until foamy. Gradually add sugar, pinch of salt and vanilla. Beat well, until stiff peaks form. Beat in cornstarch mixture. Spread over your favorite cooled pie filling. Cover to edges. Bake at 350° for 10 minutes.

Butterscotch Cookies

1 cup shortening
2 cups packed brown sugar
2 eggs
1 teaspoon baking soda
1 teaspoon cream of tartar
3 cups flour

- Preheat oven to 350°. In medium bowl, cream shortening and sugar; add eggs and beat well. Add remaining ingredients plus pinch of salt. Drop by heaping teaspoonfuls onto sprayed cooking sheets and bake for 8 to 9 minutes.

TIP: If you have raisins, dates, nuts or M&Ms on hand, throw them into the batter too! Just add 1 cup of your favorite candy or nuts.

Gooey Butter Cookies

½ cup (1 stick) butter, softened
¼ teaspoon vanilla
1 egg
1 (8 ounce) package cream cheese
1 (18 ounce) box butter recipe yellow cake mix
2 cups powdered sugar

- Preheat oven to 350°. In large bowl, combine all ingredients, except powdered sugar and beat on medium speed. Cover and chill.

- Form into balls and dip in powdered sugar. Drop balls onto sprayed cookie sheets and bake for 7 to 10 minutes or until golden brown.

Grandma's Oatmeal Cookies

1 cup (2 sticks) butter, softened
1 cup sugar
1 cup packed brown sugar
2 eggs, beaten
1 cup raisins
2 cups oatmeal
1 cup flaked coconut
1 teaspoon baking soda
1 teaspoon baking powder
2 cups flour
1 teaspoon vanilla

- Preheat oven to 350°. In large bowl, cream butter and sugars until they blend well. Add eggs and beat until smooth. Stir in raisins oatmeal and coconut.

- In small bowl, combine baking soda, baking powder, flour and ½ teaspoon salt. Pour flour mixture into sugar mixture, add vanilla and mix well.

- Drop by heaping teaspoonfuls onto sprayed, baking sheets and bake for 8 to 10 minutes. Makes about 4 dozen.

TIP: Toss in 1 cup chocolate or butterscotch chips for an added treat.

Imogene's Sugar Cookies

2 cups sugar
½ cup (1 stick) butter
2 eggs
1 teaspoon baking soda
1 teaspoon baking powder
1 teaspoon vanilla
1 teaspoon lemon juice
½ teaspoon almond extract
1 cup buttermilk*
5 cups flour

- Preheat oven to 400°. In large bowl, combine all ingredients except flour. Add ½ teaspoon salt and hand mix flour a little at a time. Chill dough. Roll out on floured board. Cut with cookie cutter and place on sprayed cookie sheet.

- Bake for 8 minutes. Cool before serving.

TIP: To make buttermilk, mix 1 cup milk with 1 tablespoon lemon juice or vinegar and let milk rest about 10 minutes.

TIP: You can ice cookies with your favorite icing, if you like.

Oatmeal Drop Cookies

2 cups sifted all-purpose flour
1 teaspoon baking soda
1½ teaspoons cinnamon
2 cups quick-cooking oatmeal
1 cup (2 sticks) butter, softened
½ cup sugar
¾ cup packed brown sugar
2 eggs, unbeaten
1½ teaspoons vanilla
⅓ cup milk
1 cup raisins
1 cup chopped dates or chocolate chips

- Preheat oven to 375°. In medium bowl, combine flour, baking soda, cinnamon and 1 teaspoon salt; add oatmeal.

- In large bowl, combine butter, sugars, eggs and vanilla. Beat on medium speed for 2 minutes; add milk. Gradually add flour mixture while beating on low speed until ingredients mix well. Add raisins and dates or chocolate chips and beat on high speed for 1½ minutes.

- Drop by heaping teaspoonfuls onto sprayed cookie sheets and bake about 12 minutes or until nicely brown. Makes about 5 dozen.

TIP: Use ¾ cup (1½ sticks) butter rather than 1 cup (2 sticks) butter to make cookies softer and chewier.

Rabbit Cookies

1½ cups (3 sticks) butter
3 cups sugar
3 eggs
1 tablespoon vanilla
5 cups flour
1 teaspoon baking soda
1 cup sour cream

- Preheat oven to 375°. In large bowl, cream butter and sugar; stir in eggs and vanilla in medium bowl, combine flour, baking soda and pinch of salt. Use mixer to add one-third flour mixture into butter and eggs and mix well. Repeat twice using one-third flour mixture each time. Stir in sour cream and refrigerate overnight.

- Take small portion at a time and roll on floured board. Cut with cookie cutter and bake on sprayed cookie sheet for 7 to 8 minutes or until light brown.

Soy is very high in protein, which is the nutrient that repairs and builds new body tissue. Soy is good for your heart and your whole body too!

Reunion Cookies

1 box whole graham crackers
⅔ cups sweetened condensed milk
⅔ cup sugar
½ cup (1 stick) butter
1 tablespoon flour
1 egg
½ cup chopped nuts
½ cup shredded coconut
1 teaspoon vanilla
1 (16 ounce) can prepared vanilla icing

- Place layer of whole graham crackers in 9 x 13-inch baking dish. In saucepan, cook milk, sugar, butter, flour and egg on medium heat until thick; stir constantly. Stir in remaining ingredients. Pour mixture over crackers in baking dish and place a second layer of whole graham crackers on top. Spread icing over top.

TIP: Add sprinkles or another topper to make these cookies an even bigger hit at your next family gathering.

Soybeans are made into fuel for buses and trucks. This is called biodiesel. Biodiesel is good for our environment, because it burns cleaner than regular diesel.

193

Old-Fashioned Ginger Snaps

4 cups flour
4 teaspoons baking soda
2 teaspoons cinnamon
1 teaspoon ground cloves
1 teaspoon ginger
1½ cups shortening
2½ cups sugar, divided
½ cup molasses
2 eggs

- Preheat oven to 325°. In medium bowl, combine flour, baking soda, cinnamon, cloves, ginger and 1 teaspoon salt. In large bowl, beat shortening and 2 cups sugar on medium speed. Add molasses and eggs and beat well. Add flour mixture to sugar mixture. Mix well, cover tightly and chill for 1 hour.

- Form into 1-inch balls and roll in remaining sugar and place about 2 inches apart onto sprayed cookie sheet and bake for 8 to 10 minutes.

Powdered Sugar Frosting:
1 teaspoon vanilla
½ teaspoon milk
3 cups powdered sugar

- In small bowl, stir vanilla and milk into powdered sugar until mixture is smooth. Drizzle over cookies while cookies are still hot. Makes about 7 dozen.

Better-Than-Ever Good Bars

2 cups flour
1 cup packed brown sugar
1 cup sugar
1 cup instant oatmeal
1 teaspoon baking powder
1 teaspoon baking soda
3 eggs, beaten
1 cup chocolate chips
1 cup oil
1 teaspoon vanilla
½ cup chopped nuts

- Preheat oven to 350°. Combine flour, brown sugar, sugar, oatmeal, baking powder, baking soda and 1 teaspoon salt in large bowl. Stir in eggs, chocolate chips, oil vanilla and nuts; mix well. Pour batter into jelly-roll pan. Bake for 20 minute and cut into squares while still hot.

Chocolate Chip Cheesecake Bars

2 (18 ounce) rolls chocolate chip cookie dough
¾ cup sugar
1 (8 ounce) package cream cheese, softened
1 egg

- Preheat oven to 375°. Spread 1 roll cookie dough in sprayed 9 x 13-inch baking dish. In blender, mix sugar, cream cheese and egg and spread mixture over dough. Drop teaspoonfuls of remaining cookie dough on top of cream cheese mixture and bake for 25 minutes.

Chocolate-Drizzled Cherry Bars

2 cups flour
2 cups quick-cooking oats
1 cup sugar
1½ cups (3 sticks) butter, softened
1 (20 ounce) can cherry pie filling
1 teaspoon almond extract
¼ cup semi-sweet chocolate chips
1 teaspoon shortening

- Preheat oven to 350°. In large bowl, combine flour, oats, sugar, and butter until crumbly. Set aside 1½ cups for topping. Press remaining crumb mixture into sprayed 9 x 13-inch baking pan. Bake for 15 to 18 minutes until edges begin to brown.

- In medium bowl, combine pie filling and extract and carefully spread over crust. Sprinkle with saved crumb mixture. Bake 20 to 25 minutes longer or until edges and topping are light brown.

- In microwave or heavy saucepan, melt chocolate chips and shortening. Stir until smooth and drizzle over warm bars. Cool completely on wire rack. Makes about 3 dozen.

Frosted Pumpkin Bars

4 eggs
1 cup oil
2 cups sugar
1 cup pumpkin
2 cups flour
2 teaspoons cinnamon
1 teaspoon baking soda
1 teaspoon baking powder

- Preheat oven to 350°. In large bowl, beat eggs and add remaining ingredients plus ½ teaspoon salt and stir until smooth. Pour into sprayed jelly-roll pan. Bake for 20 minutes or until middle is firm. Let cool before frosting. Makes 36 to 48 bars.

Cream Cheese Frosting:
1 (3 ounce) package cream cheese, softened
6 tablespoons (3/4 stick) butter
3 cups powdered sugar
1 teaspoon vanilla
1 teaspoon milk

- Combine ingredients in medium bowl and stir until smooth. Add more powdered sugar or milk as needed.

Morton, Illinois is the known as The Pumpkin Capital of the World. Illinois is the leading state in pumpkin production. They grow 16.6 million pumpkins each year.

197

Homemade Payday Candy Bars

2 (12 ounce) jars dry roasted peanuts
½ cup (1 stick) butter
2 cups mini marshmallows
1 (14 ounce) can sweetened condensed milk
1 (12 ounce) package peanut butter chips

- Layer the bottom of sprayed 9 x 13-inch pan or jelly-roll pan with 1 jar of nuts.

- In saucepan on low heat, melt butter, marshmallows and stir in milk and peanut butter chips while stirring constantly.

- Pour peanut butter mixture over layered nuts and top with second jar of peanuts. Press with fingers and allow to set until firm. Cut bars into squares and serve.

Mom's Chocolate Peanut Butter Bars

½ cup light corn syrup
¼ cup packed brown sugar
1 cup peanut butter
3 cups Cheerios
1 (6 ounce) package chocolate chips
1 teaspoon vanilla

- In saucepan bring corn syrup, sugar and ⅛ teaspoon salt to a boil. Stir in peanut butter; remove from heat. Stir in cereal, chocolate chips and vanilla until ingredients mix well. Pour into sprayed 9 x 9-inch baking pan and pat down. Refrigerate about one hour and cut into squares.

Rainbow Rocky Road Brownies

1 (18 ounce) box brownie mix
½ cup oil
2 eggs
2 cups miniature marshmallows
⅔ cup mini chocolate chips
1 cup salted peanuts
½ cup caramel ice cream topping

- Heat oven to 350 °. Spray bottom of 9 x 13-inch pan. In large bowl, combine brownie mix, ¼ cup water, oil and eggs. Beat 50 strokes with spoon. Spread in sprayed pan.

- Bake for 28 to 30 minutes. Remove pan from oven. Immediately sprinkle with marshmallows, chocolate chips and peanuts. Drizzle with caramel topping. Bake an additional 5 to 7 minutes or until marshmallows begin to puff. Cool completely. (For ease in cutting, use non-serrated knife dipped in water.) Makes 16 servings.

A single vine from pumpkin plants can grow up to 20 feet long. It takes 110 days for a pumpkin vine to produce mature pumpkins. Giant pumpkins can grow five pounds a day!

Lickin' Good
Peanut Butter Fingers

½ cup (1 stick) butter
½ cup sugar
½ cup packed brown sugar
1 egg
⅓ cup peanut butter
½ teaspoon baking soda
¼ teaspoon vanilla
1 cup flour
1 cup quick-rolled oats

- Preheat oven to 350°. Cream butter, sugar and brown sugar in large bowl. Stir in egg, peanut butter, baking soda, vanilla and pinch of salt; mix well. Gradually add flour and rolled oats. Mixture will be very stiff.

- Place in sprayed 11 x 16-inch pan. Bake for 20 to 25 minutes or until light brown.

In the early 1800's, Johnny Appleseed planted millions of apple seeds in the land between the Ohio and Mississippi Rivers. It takes fifteen years for an apple tree grown from a seed to begin producing apples.

Cashew-Caramel Brownies

1 (8 ounce) package semi-sweet chocolate chips
¼ cup butter
⅔ cup sugar
2 eggs
1 teaspoon vanilla
1 cup flour
1 cup chopped cashews
1 (8 ounce) package chocolate-caramel baking chips

- Preheat oven to 350°. Melt chocolate and butter together. Mix in sugar, eggs and vanilla. Stir in flour. Fold in cashews and chocolate-caramel chips. Spoon into sprayed 9-inch square pan and bake 20 to 25 minutes until golden brown.

Peanut Butter
Crispy Rice Treats

½ cup sugar
½ cup white corn syrup
⅔ cup peanut butter
3 cups crispy rice cereal

- In saucepan, heat sugar and syrup until sugar dissolves. Do not boil. Stir in peanut butter and crispy rice cereal and mix well. Pour mixture into 8 x 8-inch baking dish and pat down to compress treats. Cut into squares to serve.

Salted Peanut Chews

1 (18 ounce) package yellow cake mix
⅔ cup (⅔ stick) butter, softened
1 egg
3 cups mini marshmallows

- Preheat oven to 350°. In large bowl, combine cake mix, butter and egg. Mix on low speed until crumbly. Press mixture into ungreased 9 x 13-inch baking pan. Bake for 12 to 18 minutes or until golden brown. Sprinkle marshmallows on top and return to oven for 1 to 2 minutes or until marshmallows begin to puff.

Peanut Butter Topping:
⅔ cup corn syrup
¼ cup (½ stick) butter
2 teaspoons vanilla
1 (12 ounce) package peanut butter chips
2 cups corn flakes
2 cups salted peanuts

- In large saucepan, cook syrup, butter, vanilla and chips until smooth and stir constantly. Remove from heat and stir in cereal and nuts. Immediately spread warm topping over marshmallows. Chill and cut into bars. Store covered.

Blissful Blueberry Delight

Crust:
1 cup flour
1 cup chopped pecans
½ cup packed brown sugar
½ cup butter

Filling:
2 (8 ounce) packages cream cheese, softened
½ cup powdered sugar
1 teaspoon vanilla
1 (12 ounce) carton frozen whipped topping
2 (20 ounce) cans blueberry pie filling

Crust:
- Preheat oven to 350°. In bowl, combine flour, pecans and brown sugar. With fork, stir in butter until crumbly. Lightly pat into ungreased 9 x 13-inch baking pan. Bake for 18 to 20 minutes or until golden brown. Cool completely.

Filling:
- In mixing bowl, beat cream cheese, powdered sugar and vanilla until smooth. Fold in whipped topping. Carefully spread over crust and top with pie filling. Cover and refrigerate for at least 2 hours. Yields: 12 to 15 servings.

Bountiful Blueberry Squares

1 cup butter
1¾ cups sugar
4 eggs
1 teaspoon vanilla
1 teaspoon almond extract
3 cups flour
1 (20 ounce) can blueberry pie filling
1 (16 ounce) can prepared vanilla icing

- Preheat oven to 350°. Cream butter and sugar. Add eggs, one at a time and beat well after each addition until mixture is light and fluffy. Stir in vanilla and almond extract. Stir in flour and 1 teaspoon salt.

- Spread half of batter on sprayed 7 x 11-inch baking sheet with 1-inch sides. Cover with pie filling. Drop spoonfuls of remaining batter evenly over filling.

- Bake for 45 minutes. Cool. Ice squares with vanilla icing or thin icing with ⅓ cup hot water and drizzle over squares.

Thirty six states grow apples to sell, including Illinois. About 300 different varieties of apples are grown in the United States!

Cherry Crisp

Pastry:
½ cup packed brown sugar
1 cup flour
½ cup butter, softened

Filling:
1 cup sugar
¼ cup cornstarch
4 cups pitted, tart red cherries, drained, juice saved
Red food coloring

Topping:
1½ cups quick-cooking oats
½ cup packed brown sugar
¼ cup flour
5 tablespoons butter, melted

- Preheat oven to 350°. Combine ¼ teaspoon salt, sugar and flour and cut in butter. Press into 2-quart or 7 x 11-inch baking dish. Bake for 15 minutes.

- For filling, combine sugar and cornstarch in saucepan, stir in 1 cup cherry juice (if you don't have 1 cup juice, add water to make 1 cup) and cook over medium heat until thick; stir constantly. Fold in cherries and just enough food coloring for a bright color. Pour over baked crust.

- Combine all topping ingredients and sprinkle over filling. Bake for 20 to 25 minutes or until golden brown.

Cherry-Cheese Crescents

1 (8 count) package crescent rolls
1 (8 ounce) package cream cheese, softened
½ cup sugar
1 tablespoon lemon juice
1 tablespoon flour
1 (20 ounce) can cherry pie filling
2 tablespoons sugar
1 teaspoon cinnamon

- Preheat oven to 350°. Pat crescent rolls onto sprayed cookie sheet. Seal edges. Beat together cream cheese, ½ cup sugar, lemon juice and flour. Spread on dough leaving 2 inches clear on all sides.

- Spread pie filling down middle of cheese mixture. Fold sides over and pinch ends closed. Mix 2 tablespoons sugar and cinnamon together and sprinkle over top. Bake for 20 to 30 minutes.

There are approximately 7,500 varieties of apples. Apple growers produce 265 million bushels of apples per year.

Pumpkin Crunch

1 (29 ounce) can solid pumpkin
1 (12 ounce) cam evaporated milk
3 eggs
1½ cups sugar
4 teaspoons pumpkin pie spice
1 (18 ounce) package yellow cake mix
1 cup chopped pecans
1 cup (2 sticks) butter, melted

- Preheat oven to 350°. Spray 9 x 13-inch pan. Combine pumpkin, evaporated milk, eggs, sugar, spice and ½ teaspoon salt in large bowl.

- Pour into sprayed pan. Sprinkle dry cake mix evenly over pumpkin mixture. Top with pecans and drizzle with melted butter.

- Bake for 50 to 55 minutes or until golden brown. Cool completely. Serve with whipped topping.

Pumpkins are good for your body. The filling is rich in Vitamin A and potassium. Pumpkins are low in calories, fat and sodium.

207

Heavenly Dessert

1 cup flour
½ cup (1 stick) butter, softened
1 cup pecan pieces
1 (8 ounce) package cream cheese, softened
1 cup powdered sugar
1 (16 ounce) carton whipped topping, divided
2 (3 ounce) boxes chocolate instant pudding
3 cups milk

• Mix flour, butter and pecan pieces and press into sprayed 9 x 13-inch baking pan. Bake 15 minutes at 350°. Cool. Beat together cream cheese and powdered sugar and fold in 1 cup whipped topping and spread mixture on top. Mix chocolate pudding and milk and spread on cream cheese layer. Spread remaining whipped topping on top.

Chewies

⅔ cup evaporated milk, divided
1 (14 ounce) package Kraft caramels
1 (18 ounce) box yellow cake mix
5 tablespoons butter, softened
1½ cups chocolate chips

• Preheat oven to 350°. Melt ⅓ cup evaporated milk and caramels and set aside. Combine cake mix, butter and ⅓ cup evaporated milk. Place half mixture in 8 x 8-inch pan and bake for 5 minutes. Remove from oven and put caramel mixture and chocolate chips on top. Spoon on remaining cake mixture and bake for 15 minutes.

Chocolate-Cookie Ice Cream Dessert

45 chocolate sandwich cookies, crushed
4 tablespoons (½ stick) butter, melted
1 (½ gallon) ice cream, any flavor
1 (16 ounce) jar fudge topping, softened
4 - 6 toffee candy bars
1 (12 ounce) carton whipped topping

- Crush cookies and mix ½ cup crumb mixture with butter. Press into bottom of 9 x 13-inch pan and freeze. Soften ice cream slightly, spread over cookie base and freeze again.

- Spread fudge topping over ice cream, sprinkle with bits of toffee bars and freeze again. Cover with whipped topping and sprinkle with remaining cookie crumbs. Refrigerate.

Freezer Vanilla Ice Cream

Freeze and enjoy!

3 - 4 eggs, beaten
2½ cups sugar
1 tablespoon vanilla
2 quarts half-and-half cream
1½ cups milk

- Beat eggs until light and fluffy. Mix sugar and ½ teaspoon salt and gradually add to beaten eggs. Blend in vanilla. Slowly add cream and milk until mixture blends well. Freeze in an ice cream freezer. Makes 1 gallon.

Homemade Ice Cream

1 quart milk
2 cups sugar
¼ cup flour
4 eggs, slightly beaten
1 tablespoon vanilla
1½ quarts half-and-half cream

- Warm milk. Mix sugar, flour and ½ teaspoon salt. Add enough hot milk to sugar mixture to make thin paste. Stir paste into hot milk. Cook over low heat, stirring constantly, until mixture thickens slightly, about 15 minutes.

- Add beaten eggs to hot mixture gradually and cook over low heat, stirring constantly, until mixture thickens slightly, about 2 minutes. Do not cook longer or eggs may curdle.

- Cool quickly in refrigerator. Do not allow mixture to cool at room temperature. Add vanilla and cream to cooled mixture. Pour into freezer can, fill only two-thirds full to allow for expansion. Freeze.

Ice Cream

4 different flavors gelatin mix
½ gallon vanilla ice cream

- Dissolve each flavor of gelatin with 1 cup hot water in small bowl. Add ⅛ gallon ice cream to each until it dissolves. Pour into mold and freeze for 10 minutes. Repeat with each flavor layer.

Frozen Crispy Treats

2 cups (4 sticks) butter, softened
2 cups packed brown sugar
6 cups crispy rice cereal
1 (½ gallon) carton rainbow sherbet, softened

- In bowl, mix butter and brown sugar until will blended. Stir in cereal and spread in 9 x 13-inch pan. (Reserve one-fourth for topping.) Spoon softened sherbet evenly over mixture. Spread remaining cereal on top. Freeze.

Old-Fashioned Bread Pudding

¼ cup butter, softened
10 slices bread, toasted
4 eggs
½ cup sugar plus 4 teaspoons sugar, divided
2 cups evaporated milk
2 teaspoons vanilla
½ teaspoon ground cinnamon

- Butter toasted bread. Cut bread into chunks and place in sprayed 9 x 13-inch, ovenproof glass dish. Beat eggs, ½ cup sugar, milk, 2 cups water and vanilla. Pour mixture over toast and let stand 10 minutes.

- Combine remaining 4 teaspoons sugar and cinnamon and sprinkle over dish. Place dish in shallow baking pan. Bake at 325° for 1 hour or until knife inserted in center comes out clean. Remove dish from water. Serve warm.

Dorothy's Cherry Pudding

1 (10 ounce) jar cherries with juice
1½ cups sugar, divided
2 tablespoons butter, melted
½ cup milk
1 teaspoon baking powder
1 cup flour

- Drain cherries and save juice. Pour cherries into sprayed 8 x 8-inch pan. Combine ½ cup sugar with remaining ingredients in medium bowl. Pour batter over cherries. Measure cherry juice plus water to make 1 cup and pour into saucepan. Add 1 cup sugar and bring to a boil. Pour liquid over batter and bake at 350° for 30 minutes.

Scrumptious Tapioca Pudding

6 cups milk
¾ cup small pearl tapioca
1 cup sugar
4 egg yolks
1 (8 ounce) carton whipped topping
1 teaspoon vanilla

- Soak milk, tapioca, ½ teaspoon salt and sugar in large bowl for 30 minutes. Cook in microwave for 10 minutes, stir and cook another 3 minutes. Stir and cook 3 more minutes. Beat egg yolks well. Add spoonfuls of hot tapioca mixture to egg and stir well. Transfer mixture back into large bowl and cook in microwave 2 to 3 minutes and stir. Cover with plastic wrap and chill, stir occasionally. Fold in whipped topping and vanilla.

Bourbon Sauce

⅓ cup evaporated milk, chilled
¼ cup sugar
3 tablespoons bourbon
2 tablespoons sour cream

- In medium bowl, beat milk until it thickens. Slowly add sugar, bourbon and sour cream. Serve over warm bread pudding or any type of cake.

Festive Eggnog Sauce

½ cup whipping cream
2 tablespoons powdered sugar
½ cup eggnog
1 tablespoon rum or brandy, optional

- In small bowl, beat cream with sugar until stiff. Gently fold in eggnog and rum until they blend well. Cover and chill. Just before serving, gently blend again. Serve with pudding, fresh fruit cup, ice cream or over angel food cake. Makes 1½ cups.

Hot Praline Sauce

¾ cup dark corn syrup
¼ cup packed brown sugar
2 teaspoons flour
1 tablespoon butter
1 teaspoon vanilla

- In saucepan, combine all ingredients and ½ cup water. Cook over medium heat until mixture thickens.

Melt-In-Your-Mouth Hot Fudge Sauce

1 (12 ounce) package chocolate chips
1 (5 ounce) can evaporated milk
1 cup sugar
2 tablespoons (¼ stick) butter
1 teaspoon vanilla
1 tablespoon brandy, optional

- In saucepan, slowly melt chocolate chips, milk and sugar
  on medium heat until they blend well; stir constantly.
  When mixture comes to rolling boil, remove from heat and
  stir in butter, vanilla and brandy if desired. Chill. Keeps for
  2 to 3 weeks.

Schielein's Butterscotch Ice Cream Topping

1 cup sugar
½ tablespoon molasses
2 tablespoons corn syrup
1 (8 ounce) carton whipping cream
1 teaspoon vanilla
1 tablespoon butter

- Combine all ingredients plus pinch of salt in saucepan.
  Bring to boil over medium heat and stir constantly. Boil
  3 to 4 minutes and stir constantly; cool slightly. Pour into
  jars and store in refrigerator. Makes about
  12 ounces.

Delightful Vanilla Caramels

1½ cups sugar
1 cup light corn syrup
¼ cup (½ stick) butter
1 cup heavy cream
1 teaspoon vanilla

- Except vanilla, boil all ingredients with ½ teaspoon salt to 245°, stirring often. Remove from fire and add vanilla. Mix well. Pour into sprayed 8 x 12-inch pan and cool. Cut into 1-inch squares and wrap in wax paper.

Fantasy Fudge

3 cups sugar
¾ cup butter
1 (5 ounce) can evaporated milk
1 (12 ounce) package semi-sweet chocolate chips
1 (7 ounce) jar marshmallow creme
1 cup chopped nuts
1 teaspoon vanilla

- Combine sugar, butter and milk in heavy 2½-quart saucepan. Bring to a full rolling boil, stirring constantly. Continue boiling 5 minutes over medium heat, stirring constantly to prevent scorching. Remove from heat.

- Stir in chocolate pieces until melted. Add marshmallow creme, nuts and vanilla. Beat until well blended. Pour into greased 9 x 13-inch pan. Cool and cut into squares. Yields: 3 pounds.

Grandma's Fudge

1 (12 ounce) can evaporated milk
½ cup (1 stick) butter
4½ cups sugar
3 (12 ounce) packages chocolate chips
1 (7 ounce) jar marshmallow creme
1 tablespoon vanilla
½ cup pecans, optional

- In large pan, mix evaporated milk, butter and sugar on stove. Must stir constantly while bringing to a boil. Boil 8 minutes exactly while continuing to stir. Too little time and fudge will not set; too long, fudge will be grainy.

- Remove from heat. Add chocolate chips, marshmallow creme, vanilla and pecans. Beat well. Pour into a buttered 9 x 13-inch pan and spread evenly. For white fudge, leave out chocolate chips.

Million Dollar Chocolate Fudge

2 cups chopped nuts
1 (12 ounce) bar milk chocolate
2 (7 ounce) jars marshmallow creme
1(12 ounce) package chocolate chips
2 teaspoons vanilla
4½ cups sugar
1 (12 ounce) can evaporated milk
½ cup (1 stick) butter

- In a large bowl put nuts, chocolate bar, marshmallow creme, chocolate chips and vanilla. In cooking pan put sugar, milk and butter. Boil at a full rolling boil for six minutes. Pour onto mixture in bowl. Mix well. Pour into sprayed 9 x 13-inch pan. Cool and cut into squares.

Grandma's
Peanut Butter Fudge

2 cups sugar
4 tablespoons white corn syrup
½ cup (1 stick) butter
½ cup milk
1 teaspoon vanilla
1 cup peanut butter

- Mix first 4 ingredients in medium saucepan. Cook over medium heat until it boils. Stirring constantly, boil for six minutes.

- Remove from heat and add vanilla and peanut butter. Stir until peanut butter is melted.

- Pour into greased 8 x 8-inch pan (or loaf pan if you want to make slices). Let set before cutting.

TIP: Adding 2 heaping tablespoons of cocoa to the first 4 ingredients can make chocolate peanut butter fudge.

The United States produces about 900 million gallons of ice cream a year. Dolly Madison served ice cream at the second inaugural ball in 1812.

Microwave Pecan Brittle

1 cup sugar
½ cup white corn syrup
1½ cups chopped pecans
1 teaspoon butter
1 teaspoon vanilla
1 teaspoon baking soda

- In a large glass bowl mix sugar and corn syrup. Microwave on HIGH for 4 minutes. Add pecans. Microwave 4 more minutes. Add butter and vanilla and cook 2 minutes. Add baking soda and stir. Pour on greased pan quickly and spread. Wait for it to cool then break apart.

Holiday Peanut Brittle

2 cups sugar
1 cup light corn syrup
1½ cups unsalted raw peanuts
3 tablespoons butter
1 teaspoon vanilla
2 teaspoons baking soda

- Combine sugar, corn syrup and ¼ cup water in a heavy 3-quart saucepan. Mix well.

- Cook over medium heat stirring constantly until sugar dissolves. Stir frequently until mixture reaches 285°. Remove from heat at once. Stir in peanuts and butter. Cook, stirring constantly until mixture reaches 295°. Remove from heat at once.

- Add vanilla and baking soda. Stir to blend well (FAST). Mixture will foam. Pour onto sprayed sheet cake pan. This is very hot, be careful. Cool and break.

218

Zap-It Almond-Butter Crunch

½ cup (1 stick) butter
1½ cups sugar
1 tablespoon light corn syrup
½ teaspoon vanilla
4 (1.5 ounce) milk chocolate bars
½ cup finely chopped almonds

- In 3-quart baking dish, heat butter on HIGH for 1½ minutes until it melts. Stir in sugar, 3 tablespoons water and syrup. Cook on HIGH for 8 minutes, add vanilla and pour onto well sprayed sheet of wax paper.

- Put chocolate on top and spread evenly as it melts. Sprinkle with almonds and press into chocolate. Chill and break.

TIP: You can substitute pecans for almonds. Both taste wonderful!

A cow that eats grass, corn, hay and mixed feed can produce 100 glasses of milk a day. A cow's udder can hold 25-50 pounds of milk.

219

Larry's Microwave Pralines

1 (1 pound) box brown sugar
2 tablespoons light corn syrup
1 cup whipping cream
1 tablespoon butter
2 cups chopped pecans

- Combine first three ingredients in 8 cup glass measuring cup. Cook by microwave on HIGH for 13 minutes. Then add 1 tablespoon butter and 2 cups chopped pecans. Beat candy until creamy. Drop by teaspoonfuls on wax paper or pour into 8 x 8-inch buttered pan and cut into squares.

Creme Cheese Mints

1 (3 ounce) package cream cheese, softened
1 pound powdered sugar
Candy paste color
Candy flavoring

- Mash soft cream cheese. Add powdered sugar gradually. Mixture will be stiff. If you are making more than one color and flavor, separate the candy mixture into individual bowls now. Add desired candy flavoring (½ teaspoon) and candy paste coloring a little at a time until you reach the shade you want. Roll into small balls. Roll the balls in granulated sugar. Press the ball into Prue Rubber Candy Molds. Unmold at once. Candies freeze well. Makes approximately 90 candies.

COME ON KIDS!
Kids In The Kitchen

Learning to cook can be an adventure for boys and girls. Cooking is a skill, so learning the correct way the first time will ensure fun and success in the kitchen.

Have a wonderful time by following these simple rules:

1. Choose a time that suits your mother or father.
2. Wash your hands.
3. Read the recipe and all the directions before you begin.
4. Gather all ingredients, utensils and pans before you begin.
5. Read the recipe again. Don't leave anything out!
6. Leave the kitchen spic and span.
7. Have fun and enjoy!

Too Good Taco Dip

1 pound ground beef
1 (15 ounce) can chili without beans
½ (8 ounce) package cubed processed cheese

- Brown ground beef and drain well. Add chili and cheese and cook on low heat until cheese melts; stir often. Serve with taco chips or serve on French bread.

TIP: If you'd rather cook this dip in the oven, bake at 350° for 30 minutes.

Awesome Apple Dip

1 (8 ounce) package cream cheese, softened
1 cup packed brown sugar
1 teaspoon vanilla
Apples

- Combine cream cheese, sugar and vanilla in small bowl. Spread dip on apple slices.

B.L.T. Dip

1 (16 ounce) package bacon
1 (8 ounce) package cream cheese, softened
1 cup salad dressing
1 large tomato, diced, drained
1 loaf bread

- Cook bacon until crisp, drain and crumble. Save bacon drippings and set aside. Combine cream cheese and salad dressing in bowl and fold in tomatoes and bacon gently. Pour just enough bacon dripping in cream cheese mixture to give it a "BLT" flavor. Toast bread and cut into bite-size pieces for dipping.

Very Best Veggie Dip

1 (1 ounce) packet ranch-style dressing mix
2 (8 ounce) packages cream cheese, softened

- Beat together dressing and cream cheese in medium bowl. Add milk for desired consistency. Chill until ready to serve.

Cheesy Chili Dip

1 pound ground beef
1 (15 ounce) can chili beans
1 (16 ounce) package shredded processed cheese
Chili powder

- Brown ground beef and drain. Add beans and cheese and cook on medium heat until cheese melts and stir often. Add chili powder to taste.

Chili-Cheese Dip

1 (8 ounce) package cream cheese, softened
1 (15 ounce) can chili without beans
1 (16 ounce) package shredded colby Jack cheese
1 (10 ounce) bag corn chips

- Spread cream cheese in bottom of microwave-safe dish. Spoon chili over cream cheese and sprinkle cheese on top.

- Microwave for 4 minutes or until cheese melts. Serve with corn chips.

224

Shrimply Delicious Chip Dip

1 (8 ounce) carton sour cream
1 cup mayonnaise
1 (6 ounce) can shrimp, chopped
1 (4 ounce) package shredded cheddar cheese
Garlic salt
Onion salt

- Combine all ingredients in large bowl and chill. Serve with chips or crackers.

Popeye's Spinach Dip

1 (16 ounce) carton sour cream
1 cup mayonnaise
2 (10 ounce) packages frozen spinach, thawed,
   drained well
1 (1 ounce) packet dry vegetable soup mix
1 cup chopped green onions
1 loaf Hawaiian bread

- In large bowl, mix sour cream and mayonnaise. Add spinach, soup mix and green onions and mix well. Chill overnight.

- Cut bread from center into bite-size pieces and serve with dip. Pour dip into bread shell or large platter and arrange bread pieces around dip.

Fluffy Peanut Butter Dip

½ cup creamy peanut butter
1 (8 ounce) carton vanilla yogurt
⅛ teaspoon ground cinnamon
½ cup whipped topping
Apples or pears

- Whisk peanut butter, yogurt and cinnamon in medium bowl until mixture blends well. Use whisk to gently stir whipped topping into peanut butter mixture until it blends well. Place dip in bowl for serving and use fruit for dipping.

Fluffy Strawberry Dip

1 (8 ounce) carton strawberry yogurt
⅛ teaspoon ground cinnamon
½ cup whipped topping
Apples or pears

- Whisk yogurt and cinnamon in medium bowl until mixture blends well. Use whisk to gently stir in whipped topping. Pour dip into bowl for serving and use fruit for dipping.

Blueberry Smoothie

2 cups blueberries
1 cup pineapple juice
1 (8 ounce) carton vanilla yogurt
2 teaspoons sugar

- In blender, combine all ingredients and blend until smooth. Serve immediately.

Fruit Basket Upset

1 (8 ounce) can fruit cocktail
2 bananas, peeled, sliced
1 small apple, cubed
½ cup seedless green grapes, halved
½ cup strawberries, sliced
5 maraschino cherries with juice, quartered
¼ cup miniature marshmallows
½ cup whipping cream

- Combine all ingredients except whipping cream in large bowl. In small bowl, beat whipping cream with 2 teaspoons cherry juice for color. Fold cream into fruit bowl. Spoon salad into serving bowl and trim with extra fruit. Makes 4 to 6 servings.

Cereal Crunch

2 cups fruit-flavored cereal
2 cups crispy rice cereal
1 cup chopped nuts
1 cup miniature colored marshmallows
1½ pounds almond bark (white chocolate)

- Combine all ingredients except almond bark in large bowl. Melt almond bark in microwave and pour over mixture; stir well. Drop on wax paper by teaspoonfuls and cool.

Cocoa Continental

2 tablespoons cocoa powder
3 tablespoons sugar
2 cups milk
Marshmallows

- Combine cocoa, sugar and ⅛ teaspoon salt in saucepan. Stir in ½ cup water and bring to boil on low heat. Boil for 2 minutes and stir constantly. Stir in milk, heat on low heat and do not boil. Drop marshmallow into each cup and pour hot cocoa over it. Makes 4 servings.

TIP: Peppermint candy or whipped cream is also a very nice treat to top off your special cocoa.

S'mores Bars

8 - 10 whole graham crackers
1 (18 ounce) package brownie mix
2 cups miniature marshmallows
1 cup semi-sweet chocolate chips
⅔ cup chopped peanuts

- Preheat oven to 350°. Arrange graham crackers in single layer in greased 9 x 13-inch baking pan. Prepare brownie mix according to package directions and spread over crackers. Bake for 25 to 30 minutes or until toothpick inserted in center comes out clean.

- Sprinkle with marshmallows, chocolate chips and peanuts and bake 5 minutes longer or until marshmallows are golden brown. Cool on wire rack before cutting.

Fruity Cereal Bars

¼ cup (½ stick) butter
1 (10.5 ounce) package miniature marshmallows
6 cups fruit-flavored cereal

- Heat butter in large glass bowl in microwave until butter melts. Stir in marshmallows and coat with butter. Heat in microwave about 1 minute and stir until smooth.

- Add cereal and mix. Press mixture firmly into 9 x 13-inch pan and chill 1 hour in refrigerator. Cut into squares and store in cool place.

Fabulous French Toast

2 eggs
½ cup milk
6 slices slightly dry bread

- Heat lightly sprayed skillet or griddle. Beat eggs, milk and ¼ teaspoon salt in bowl with rotary egg beater. Dip both sides of bread in egg mixture with fork and place bread in hot skillet or griddle. Brown on both sides and turn with pancake spatula.

- Sprinkle with powdered sugar and top with butter or your favorite syrup or jelly. Serve hot.

Puppy Chow

½ cup (1 stick) butter
1 cup peanut butter
1 (12 ounce) package chocolate chips
1 (12 ounce) box Crispix® cereal
Powdered sugar

- Melt butter, peanut butter and chocolate chips in large mixing bowl in microwave. Add cereal and mix well. Spoon into resealable plastic bags, add 2 to 3 cups powdered sugar and shake well.

Kendall's Crackerjack

½ pound (two sticks) butter
6 tablespoons white corn syrup
½ teaspoon cream of tartar
2 cups packed brown sugar
1 teaspoon baking soda
8 quarts popped popcorn

- Combine in heavy pan butter, corn syrup, cream of tartar, brown sugar and ½ teaspoon salt, bring to a light/moderate boil and cook to soft/medium ball stage. (Test by dropping some in cup of lukewarm water.)

- Add baking soda. The mixture will froth up. Stir vigorously. In large roaster pan, pour frothing mixture over popped corn.

- Stir quickly to distribute the mixture. Bake at 250° for 40 to 45 minutes, stirring every 15 minutes.

The most common breed of dairy cow found in the U.S. is called Holsteins. Dairy cows weigh about 1400 pounds.

Freezer Bag Ice Cream

1 cup milk
1 cup whipping cream or half-and-half cream
¼ cup sugar
½ teaspoon vanilla

Additional Materials Needed:
1 quart and 1 gallon resealable plastic freezer bags
Duct tape
Crushed ice (about 1 bag per 3 bags ice cream)
1 cup rock salt (about 8 cups per 5 pounds)
Bath towel

- Pour milk, cream, sugar and vanilla in 1-quart freezer bag and seal. To secure bag, fold a piece of duct tape over seal. Place bag with ingredients inside a 1-gallon freezer bag. Pack larger bag with crushed ice around smaller bag and pour ¾ to 1 cup salt evenly over ice. Wrap in bath towel and shake for 10 minutes.

- Open outer bag, remove inner bag and wipe so salt water doesn't get into ice cream. Cut top and spoon into cups. Makes about 3 cups. Serve plain or top with nuts, coconut or fruit. Enjoy!

- I have used this recipe with all ages of people, from kindergarteners to adults. Everyone has fun and the end result is very tasty. It is fun for birthday parties, reunions and other special occasions. I have used it in many "Ag in the Classroom" presentations.

Marshmallow Puffs

¼ cup (½ stick) butter, melted
16 large marshmallows
1 teaspoon cinnamon
2 (8 ounce) packages crescent dinner rolls
¼ cup powdered sugar

- Preheat oven to 375°. Melt butter. Dip marshmallows in butter and then cinnamon. Wrap crescent rolls firmly around each marshmallow, starting at smallest corner.

- Dip crescent roll in butter and place in muffin pan. Bake for 10 to 15 minutes. Top with powdered sugar.

Pigs In A Sleeping Bag

¾ pound bacon
1 package hot dogs
1 (8 ounce) can crushed pineapple with juice
1 cup packed brown sugar

- Wrap bacon around hot dog and secure with toothpick and set in baking dish. Pour pineapple and juice over hot dogs and sprinkle with brown sugar. Bake at 375° for about 45 minutes.

Coney Island Hot Dogs

6 sliced frankfurter buns
6 frankfurters
1 (8 ounce) can chili con carne
2 tablespoons ketchup

- Preheat oven to 325°. Butter buns, wrap in aluminum foil and heat in oven for 15 minutes. In covered saucepan, boil 2 cups water and drop in frankfurters. Lower heat to medium and cook 5 to 8 minutes.

- Heat chili con carne and ketchup in saucepan and stir constantly. Place 1 frankfurter in each bun and cover with hot chili mixture or your favorite condiments – mustard, ketchup or pickle relish.

Peanut Butter Playdough
This treat is edible playdough.
Children can mold, make funs shapes and eat it too!

3½ cups peanut butter
4 cups powdered sugar
3½ cups honey
4 cups dry milk powder

- In large bowl, cream peanut butter and powdered sugar; stir in honey and milk powder. Divide into 15 equal portions and refrigerate or freeze until ready to use.

234

THAT'S A BIG SPREAD
Quantity Cooking

Prom Punch

1 packet raspberry drink mix
1 packet cherry drink mix
1 (6 ounce) can frozen orange juice concentrate
1 (6 ounce) can frozen lemonade concentrate
2 cups sugar
1 quart ginger ale, chilled

• Mix all ingredients except ginger ale with 3 quarts water and freeze in old ice cream bucket or equivalent. When ready to serve, pour ginger ale over frozen mixture.

Autumn Punch

1½ quarts apple juice
2 cinnamon sticks
8 whole cloves
1⅓ cups pineapple juice
½ cup lemon juice
1 quart orange juice
28 ounces ginger ale
1 large orange, sliced
2 large oranges, sliced, quartered

• Pour apple juice in large pot. Tie cinnamon sticks and cloves in cheesecloth. Add to pot and simmer, uncovered, for 15 minutes. Remove spice bag and chill. Mix spiced juice with remaining fruit juices. To serve, place a large block of ice in a punch bowl, add fruit juice combination and ginger ale. Float orange slices in punch bowl. Place ¼ slice on the edge of each punch cup. Yields: 20 servings.

Vegetable Soup

10 pound beef roast
5 pounds onions, chopped
10 pounds potatoes, peeled, chopped
1 head cabbage, chopped
5 pounds carrots, chopped
2 bunches celery, chopped
2 (15 ounce) cans whole kernel corn
2 (15 ounce) cans peas
2 (15 ounce) cans cut green beans
6 quarts tomato juice

- Cook and bone roast. Add all ingredients and cook on low heat in large soup pot for 3 hours. Makes 2 roasters.

Elizabeth's Spicy Chili

3 pounds lean ground beef
2 onions, chopped
5 (10 ounce) cans diced tomatoes with green chilies
4 (15 ounce) cans chili
2 tablespoons chili powder
6 swigs hot sauce
1 (7 ounce) can chopped green chilies

- Brown ground beef, drain. Add onions, tomatoes and green chilies, chili, 4 cups water, chili powder and hot sauce. Start with 1 teaspoon salt and add to taste. Add chopped green chilies. Cook in large pot on low for about 45 minutes to 1 hour. Stir occasionally to keep from sticking.

Chili

6 pounds ground chuck
4 onions, chopped
4 (15 ounce) cans diced tomatoes
1 (48 ounce) can tomato juice
6 (15 ounce) cans chili beans
1 (16 ounce) jar thick-and-chunky salsa
3 tablespoons chili powder

- In skillet, brown ground chuck with onions and drain. Add tomatoes, tomato juice, beans and salsa. Season with salt, pepper and chili powder.

Party-Macaroni Salad

1 (1 pound) package macaroni, cooked, drained
½ cup finely chopped broccoli
½ cup finely chopped carrots
½ cup finely chopped cauliflower
½ cup finely chopped celery
½ cup finely chopped green onion
1 (8 ounce) can peas, drained

Dressing
1 (14 ounce) can sweetened condensed milk
2 cups mayonnaise
½ cup vinegar

- Mix macaroni and vegetables; add dressing. Let stand over night.

TIP: Toss in any of your favorite veggies to this salad! You can adjust the amount of dressing depending on the amount of vegetables you add.

Pasta Salad

1½ cups oil
1½ cups sugar
1½ cups vinegar
1 tablespoon garlic salt
1 (1 pound) package pasta, cooked, drained
1 bunch fresh broccoli, chopped
1 head cauliflower, chopped
1 (12 ounce) package shredded mozzarella cheese
2 (14 ounce) cans sliced black olives

- Mix oil, sugar, vinegar, garlic salt and 1½ teaspoons pepper. Add dressing to pasta, vegetables, cheese and olives. Mix well and chill several hours before serving.

Broccoli Salad Supreme

10 cups broccoli florets
6 cups seedless red grapes
1 cup sliced celery
6 green onions, sliced
2 cups mayonnaise
⅔ cup sugar
2 tablespoons cider vinegar
1 pound bacon, cooked crisp, crumbled
1⅓ cups slivered almonds

- In large bowl, combine broccoli, grapes, celery and onions. In small bowl, combine mayonnaise, sugar and vinegar, pour over broccoli mixture and toss to coat.

- Cover and chill for at least 4 hours. Before serving, toss with bacon and almonds. Makes about 20 servings.

Bacon-Broccoli Pasta Salad

3 (12 ounce) boxes rainbow rotini pasta
1 bunch broccoli, chopped
1 bunch cauliflower, chopped
1 (12 ounce) package shredded mozzarella cheese
2 - 3 pounds bacon, fried crisp, crumbled

Dressing:
6 cups mayonnaise
3 cups sugar
1½ cups vinegar

- Prepare pasta according to package directions and cool. Combine salad ingredients in large bowl. In medium bowl, combine dressing ingredients. Pour over salad and chill. Serves 25 to 30 people.

Cherry Cola Salad

2 (20 ounce) cans cherry pie filling
2 (20 ounce) cans crushed pineapple with juice
2 (6 ounce) boxes cherry gelatin mix
1 cup chopped nuts
2 cups cola

- In saucepan, boil pie filling in 2 cups water. Remove from heat and stir in remaining ingredients. Pour into 2 (9 x 13-inch) baking pans and chill for several hours.

Sensational Slaw

4 heads cabbage, diced
2 cups shredded carrots
1 onion, chopped

Dressing:
1 quart mayonnaise
1 cup oil
1½ cups sugar
1 cup vinegar

- Mix cabbage, carrots and onion. Mix all dressing ingredients with 2 teaspoons each of salt and pepper and add to cabbage mixture. Chill.

Old-Fashioned Baked Beans

4 gallons pork and beans
1 (44 ounce) bottle ketchup
4 pounds brown sugar
1 (16 ounce) jar barbecue sauce
1¾ cups chopped onion
2½ pounds bacon, fried crisp, crumbled

- Combine all ingredients in slow cooker, stir and cook on LOW for about 5 hours.

TIP: This recipe is perfect for family reunions and serves 100 to 125 people.

Beets with Orange Sauce

1 cup sugar
½ cup cornstarch
1 (6 ounce) can frozen orange juice concentrate,
  thawed
½ cup lemon juice
¼ cup (½ stick) butter
8 (15 ounce) cans sliced beets, drained

- Combine sugar, cornstarch and 1 tablespoon salt in saucepan. Stir in orange juice and 2½ cups water. Cook and stir constantly until mixture thickens. Stir in lemon juice and butter.

- Pour sauce over beets and heat thoroughly. Makes 25 servings (about ⅓ cup each).

Make-Ahead Mashed Potatoes

12 pounds yukon gold potatoes, cubed
2 (8 ounce) packages cream cheese
1 (1 pint) carton sour cream
1 cup milk
4 teaspoons onion salt

- Preheat oven to 325°. Place potatoes in large soup pot with lightly salted water. Bring to a boil, cook until tender, drain and mash. Add remaining ingredients plus pepper to taste. Transfer to large roasting pan, cover and bake for about 1 hour.

Texas Party Potatoes

1 (16 ounce) carton sour cream
1 (8 ounce) carton sour cream
1 (16 ounce) shredded sharp cheddar cheese
5 (10 ounce) cans of cream of chicken soup
¼ cup dried onion flakes
6 pounds shredded hash brown potatoes
½ cup (1 stick) butter, melted
2 cups crushed corn flakes

- In large container combine sour creams, cheese, soup, onion flakes and 1 teaspoon salt and ½ teaspoon pepper. Add potatoes and mix well.

- Pour mixture into full-size steam-table pan and level ingredients. Mix butter and spread evenly over potatoes. Sprinkle corn flakes over top and bake at 375° for 1½ hours.

Scalloped Sweet Potatoes with Apples

10 pounds sweet potatoes
3 pounds tart apples, sliced
1 (1 pound) package brown sugar
1 cup sugar
1 cup (2 sticks) butter, sliced

- Cook potatoes, peel and slice. Spray several large baking pans and arrange alternate layers of potatoes, apples, sugars and butter. Add 2 teaspoons salt and bake at 350° for 45 minutes to 1 hour. Yields: 50 servings.

No-Fuss Chicken

1 cup apricot preserves
2 (16 ounce) bottles Russian salad dressing
2 (1 ounce) packets dry onion soup mix
24 boneless skinless chicken breast halves

- Heat preserves in microwave on HIGH for 20 to 30 seconds before mixing with other ingredients. In medium bowl, combine preserves, dressing, soup mix and ¼ cup water.

- Place chicken in 3 (9 x 13-inch) baking pans and top each with dressing mixture. Cover and bake at 350° for 25 minutes. Uncover, baste and continue baking for 25 to 35 minutes. Serve with hot, cooked rice.

Chicken-Spaghetti Casserole

3 (2 - 3 pounds) chickens
4 cups chopped celery and onion
3 (16 ounce) packages uncooked spaghetti
6 (10 ounce) cans cream of mushroom soup
3 (4 ounce) cans sliced mushrooms, drained
3 (8 ounce) packages shredded cheddar cheese

- Preheat oven to 350°. Cook chicken in large soup pot for 40 minutes. Remove chicken to cool. Save broth in pot and bone chicken. Add celery, onion and spaghetti and boil for 10 minutes.

- Add chicken, soup and mushrooms and stir. Pour mixture in 3 (9 x 13-inch) baking dishes; sprinkle with cheese. Bake for 20 minutes.

Four Pasta Beef Bake

8 cups uncooked pasta (four different shapes)
2 pounds ground beef
2 green bell peppers and onions, chopped
2 cups fresh mushrooms, sliced
4 (26 ounce) jars meatless spaghetti sauce, divided
2 eggs, lightly beaten
1 (16 ounce) package shredded mozzarella cheese

- Cook pasta according to package. In large skillet cook beef, green peppers, onions and mushrooms over medium heat until meat is no longer pink. Drain. Drain pasta and place in large bowl. Stir in beef mixture, two jars spaghetti sauce and eggs. Transfer to two sprayed 13 x 9 x 2 baking dishes. Top with remaining sauce.

- Bake uncovered at 350° for 25 minutes. Sprinkle with cheese and return to oven for 5 minutes.

Dad's Favorite Cheeseburger Bake

10 pounds ground beef
1 (1 gallon) can tomato sauce
1 (12 ounce) package shredded cheddar cheese
8 - 10 (10 count) cans biscuits

- In skillet, brown and drain meat. Return meat to skillet and add tomato sauce; simmer for 25 minutes. Pour into 2 sprayed 9 x 13-inch baking pans and cover with cheese. Place biscuits on top and bake at 350° for 15 minutes.

Crowd-Size Spaghetti Sauce

4 pounds ground beef
4 large onions, chopped
4 garlic cloves, minced
4 (28 ounce) cans diced tomatoes with liquid
½ cup fresh minced parsley
2 (15 ounce) cans tomato paste
2 (4 ounce) cans chopped ripe olives, drained
¼ cup packed brown sugar
4 teaspoons dried oregano
1 (8 ounce) can tomato sauce
2 (4 ounce) cans mushrooms, drained
2 tablespoons dried basil

- In several large soup pots, cook beef, onions and garlic over medium heat and drain. Add remaining ingredients plus 2 tablespoons salt and 2 teaspoons pepper and 2 cups water. Cover, simmer for 4 hours and stir occasionally.

Barbecue

2 small bunches celery, finely chopped
8 - 9 pounds ground beef
2 pounds onions
52 - 56 ounces ketchup
1 cup packed brown sugar

- Saute celery in butter until tender. Brown ground beef and onions; drain. Add remaining ingredients and salt to taste and simmer for at least 2 hours. May freeze. Makes 50 servings.

Spicy Country Barbecue

5 pounds ground beef
2 cups chopped onion
1 cup chopped celery
½ cup packed brown sugar
1 (10 ounce) can tomato sauce
¼ cup white vinegar
1 tablespoon Worcestershire sauce

- Brown ground beef and onion in large skillet and drain. Add remaining ingredients plus 1 tablespoon salt and ¼ teaspoon pepper. Simmer for 1 hour or longer. Yields: approximately 30 servings.

Meat Loaf for 60

20 pounds ground beef
8 eggs, lightly beaten
4 cups old-fashioned oats
2½ cups tomato juice
3 tablespoons chopped onions

Sauce:
1 cup ketchup
3 tablespoons vinegar
1 tablespoon prepared mustard
1 tablespoon brown sugar

- Preheat oven to 350°. Combine beef, eggs, oats, tomato juice, onions, 3 tablespoons salt and 1 tablespoon pepper. Form into 8 loaves and place in 9 x 5 x 3-inch loaf pans. Combine sauce ingredients and pour 3 tablespoons over each loaf. Bake for 1½ to 2 hours and baste once with remaining sauce.

Meatballs

2 (28 ounce) packages frozen meatballs
1 (12 ounce) bottle chili sauce
1 (16 ounce) jar grape jelly

- Combine all ingredients in slow cooker and cook on HIGH for 2 hours or bake in oven at 375° for 40 minutes.

Hamburger BBQ

20 pounds ground beef, browned and drained
10 medium onions, chopped
1½ cups chopped celery
1½ cups chopped green pepper
1½ gallon ketchup
10 medium onions or use onion flakes
½ cup vinegar
¼ cup Worcestershire sauce
3⅓ tablespoons chili powder
1 pound brown sugar

- In soup pot, brown beef with onion, celery and pepper. Place remaining ingredients plus 4 tablespoons salt in several large baking dishes and cook in oven at 250° for 3 hours.

Italian Roast Beef

1 (10 pound) beef roast
**2 (8 or 16 ounce) bottles fat-free Italian salad
   dressing**
1 (1 ounce) packet dry onion soup mix
2 pounds fresh mushrooms, sliced

- Put beef in roasting pan and pour salad dressing over meat. Sprinkle soup mix on top. Bake at 300° for 4 to 6 hours until meat falls apart. Add mushrooms to meat broth and heat thoroughly. Add 1 to 2 more bottles salad dressing, if desired.

Pork Chops and Sauerkraut

24 (1-inch) thick pork chops, trimmed
6 - 7 quarts sauerkraut
1 - 2 pounds bacon
4 - 5 large onions, sliced
8 (12 ounce) cans beer

- Brown chops and in skillet and season with salt and pepper. Drain sauerkraut well. Line large roasting pan with bacon and a little sauerkraut, top with layers of chops and place 1 onion slice on each chop. Cover with layer of sauerkraut.

- Add second layer of chops and top with onions and sauerkraut and enough beer to cover. Cook on 350° until bubbly on sides of pan; lower heat to 250° and cook for 3 hours or until chops are tender.

Ham Barbecue

2 (2- 3 pound) smoked ham
½ cup chopped onion
2 tablespoons oil
2 tablespoons brown sugar
½ cup ketchup
½ cup vinegar
1 tablespoon Worcestershire sauce

- Cook ham in slow cooker with ⅔ cup water on LOW for 8 to 10 hours. In large soup pot, saute onion in oil, add other ingredients and cook for 10 minutes. Shred ham and add to soup pot. Serve on rolls or buns.

Ham Loaf

5 pounds ground ham
4 pounds ground pork
2 pounds ground beef
6 eggs
4 cups milk
6 cups graham cracker crumbs

Basting ingredients:
1½ cups vinegar
4 (10 ounce) cans tomato soup
4 tablespoons dry mustard
3½ cups packed brown sugar

- In large bowl, combine ham, pork and beef together. Add eggs, milk and graham cracker crumbs and mix well. Form into 3 loaves and place on baking pan. Bake at 350° for 1 to 1½ hours. While ham loaf is baking, combine basting ingredients in saucepan and bastes loaves occasionally.

Country Corn Relish

4 quarts (about 20 ears) fresh corn
5 cups (about 6) seeded, diced green bell peppers
5 cups (about 6) seeded, diced red bell peppers
3 cups (about 4) chopped onions
1 large head cabbage, chopped
6 cups vinegar
4 cups sugar
2 tablespoons ground mustard
2 tablespoons celery seed
1 tablespoon ground tumeric

- Combine all ingredients with 1 cup water and 2 tablespoon salt in large soup pot. Simmer uncovered for 20 minutes and stir occasionally. Makes 16 pints.

Process for Preserving Relish:
- Sterilize jars and lids in simmering water.

- Lift jar from hot water with tongs. Fill with hot pickle mixture to within ½-inch of top. Wipe rim of jar with clean cloth.

- Place lid and ring on jar. Tighten.

- When cool, check lid for successful seal: Press the middle of the lid. If it springs up when released, the lid is not sealed. Refrigerate unsealed jar to prevent spoilage.

Gardener's Salsa

1¾ cups white vinegar
24 cups (12 pounds) tomatoes, peeled, quartered
½ cup hot chili peppers, diced
1½ cups sweet green peppers, finely diced
1½ cups onion, finely diced
4 ribs celery, diced
1 tablespoon sugar, optional

- Combine vinegar and tomatoes in large soup pot and cook until tender. Mash tomatoes, but leave some chunks. Add rest of ingredients and 1 tablespoon salt. Simmer until thickens, at least 1 hour. Taste and adjust seasonings.

- Ladle into hot sterile jars. Seal and put in hot water bath for 15 minutes. Instead of jars you can put salsa in containers and freeze.

TIP: You can add a little red food coloring to enhance color if you want and use a little cornstarch to thicken if the salsa it is not thick enough for you.

Illinois has about 114,000 dairy cows that produce more than two million pounds of milk a year. On average, a cow is milked 2 to 3 times a day. All female dairy cows must have a calf to produce milk.

Cornbread For A Crowd

3½ cups cornmeal
2½ cups all-purpose flour
2 tablespoons baking powder
1½ teaspoons baking soda
4 eggs
3 cups buttermilk*
1 cup vegetable oil

- Preheat oven to 425°. In large bowl, combine cornmeal, flour, baking powder, baking soda and 1½ teaspoons salt. In medium bowl, combine eggs, buttermilk and oil; pour into dry ingredients and stir until they are moist.

- Pour into greased 9 x 13-inch baking pan and greased 9-inch square baking pan. Bake for 20 to 25 minutes or until toothpick inserted near center comes out clean.

TIP: To make buttermilk, mix 1 cup milk with 1 tablespoon lemon juice or vinegar and let milk rest about 10 minutes.

Corn oil is used for cooking. It is low in cholesterol and saturated fat. Nearly one third of our nation's corn crop is exported to other countries.

Piecrust

5 pounds packages flour
1 (16 ounce) can butter-flavored shortening

- Combine flour with 2 tablespoons salt and cut in shortening. Mixture will resemble cornmeal. Add 2 cups cold water all at once and mix gently until flour absorbs water. Do not over mix. Roll into 20 balls and roll each one into 9-inch pie plate. Freeze or bake each one at 350° for 10 to 15 minutes. Yields: 10 double crusts.

TIP: If you want to make your piecrust ahead of time, this crust freezes well.

O'Bars

2¼ cups firmly packed brown sugar
1½ cups sugar
1½ cups (3 sticks) butter, softened
1½ tablespoons vanilla
3 eggs
5¼ cups flour
1 tablespoon baking soda
1 cup chocolate chips
1 cup butterscotch chips
1 cup plain M&Ms
1 cup mini marshmallows

- Preheat oven to 375°. In large bowl, beat brown sugar, sugar and butter until light and fluffy. Add vanilla and eggs; beat well. Add flour and baking soda; mix well. Stir in remaining ingredients and place on sprayed baking pan and bake for 15 to 20 minutes.

FARMERS MARKET
Pickles
Sauces

Old-Fashioned Sweet Pickles

4 quarts thinly sliced cucumbers
6 medium white onions, sliced
1 green bell pepper, julienned
1 red bell pepper, julienned
3 cups distilled white vinegar
5 cups sugar
1½ teaspoons turmeric
1½ teaspoons celery seed
2 tablespoons mustard seed

• Mix cucumbers, onions, bell peppers and ⅓ cup salt with ice cubes in large pan. Let stand for 3 hours. Drain. Combine remaining ingredients and pour liquids over cucumber mixture. Bring to a boil. Place in sterile jars and seal.

Bread & Butter Pickles

12 cucumbers, sliced
7 cups cider vinegar
7 cups sugar
2 tablespoons celery seed
3 tablespoons mustard seed
1 tablespoon turmeric
4 medium onions, cut in rings
4 green peppers, cut in strips or chopped
1 red bell pepper, cut in strips or chopped

• Soak cucumbers overnight in 6 quarts water and 1 cup salt. Drain in the morning. Bring 2 cups water, vinegar, sugar, celery seed, mustard seed and turmeric to a boil in large pot. Add cucumbers, onions, bell peppers and boil for 5 minutes. Pack in hot sterile jars and seal with flat metal lids.

Delicious Dill Pickles

Whole cloves
Flower dill
Garlic cloves
Cucumbers, small or cut in spears
2 quarts vinegar
1 cup coarse salt

- Place 1 clove, 1 dill and 1 garlic in each jar. Wash and place cucumbers in jar. Bring vinegar, 1-quart water and coarse salt to a boil, pour over cucumbers and seal with flat metal lids. Ready to eat in 6 days.

Ready-To-Eat Pickles

1 tablespoon celery seed
7 cups sliced dill pickles (about 10, 4-inch pickles)
1 cup diced onions
1 cup diced green bell peppers, sliced
1 cup vinegar
2 cups sugar

- Sprinkle celery seed and 1 tablespoon salt over pickles, onions and peppers. Let stand 1 hour and drain. Blend vinegar and sugar until sugar dissolves and pour over pickle mixture. Place in jars and chill. Pickles keep for 4 to 5 months.

Easy Pickled Jalapeno Peppers

1½ - 2 cups dill pickle juice
3 thin slices of onion (optional)
1 thin sliver of garlic (optional)
10 - 12 fresh jalapeno peppers

- Save juice from dill pickles to make these delicious peppers. Always wear gloves when handling raw jalapenos. Bring pickle juice, onion, and garlic to a boil.

- Remove stem end from peppers. Cut in half lengthwise. Scoop out seeds. Put peppers in pot pushing down into juice. Return to boiling for 1 minute. Remove from heat. Allow to cool.

Pickled Beets

4 quarts small beets
3 cups vinegar
2½ cups sugar
2 teaspoons allspice
1-inch stick whole cinnamon
½ teaspoon whole cloves

- Cook beets until tender and peel skins. Combine vinegar, 2 cups water, sugar and spices and in pot. Bring to a boil and simmer 15 minutes. Add beets and simmer 5 minutes longer. Pack beets in jar. Bring liquid back to boil and pour over beets until covered.

Basic White Sauce

White sauce is one of the basic sauces used in cooking.
It is also called bechamel sauce.

2 tablespoons butter
2 tablespoons all-purpose flour
1 cup milk

- Melt butter in saucepan over medium heat. Add flour and 1 teaspoon salt and blend. Add milk all at once and stir constantly until mixture thickens. Cook for 1 minute. Makes 1 cup.

Best-Ever BBQ Sauce

1 cup ketchup
¼ cup packed brown sugar
1 tablespoon lemon juice
1 tablespoon vinegar
2 tablespoons Worcestershire sauce
2 tablespoons hot sauce, optional

- Combine all ingredients with 2 tablespoons water and pepper to taste. Chill until ready to use.

Shrimp Cocktail Sauce

⅔ cup chili sauce
⅔ cup ketchup
⅓ cup prepared horseradish
1½ tablespoons Worcestershire sauce
1 tablespoon lemon juice

- Blend all ingredients and chill.

Special Spaghetti Sauce

This sauce is also great on lasagna. You'll love it.

2 pounds ground beef
1 cup chopped onion
2 cloves garlic, minced
3 tablespoons butter or cooking oil
2 (6 ounce) cans tomato paste
2 (8 ounce) cans tomato sauce
1 teaspoon sugar
1½ teaspoons oregano
½ teaspoon Italian seasoning
2 tablespoons dried parsley
1 bay leaf
Spaghetti, cooked

- In large heavy pot, combine ground beef, onion and garlic and cook until meat crumbles and onion is tender; drain. Add remaining ingredients plus 2 cups water and 1 teaspoon salt. Simmer, uncovered, for about 2½ to 3 hours or until sauce is thick; stir occasionally.

- Remove bay leaf. Serve over hot spaghetti.

TIP: Mushrooms may be added during the last 15 minutes of cooking.

Cranberry Spread

1 (8 ounce) package cream cheese, softened
2 tablespoons frozen orange juice concentrate,
  thawed
1 tablespoon sugar
⅛ teaspoon cinnamon
¼ cup finely chopped dried cranberries
¼ cup finely chopped pecans

- In small bowl, beat cream cheese, orange juice, sugar and cinnamon at medium speed until fluffy. Stir in cranberries and pecans and chill for 1 hour.

Cranberry Chutney

4 cups fresh cranberries
3 oranges, divided
2 granny Smith apples, peeled, chopped
1 medium onion, chopped
1½ cups packed light brown sugar
⅔ cup cider vinegar
½ cup chopped dried apricot
½ teaspoon ground nutmeg
2 cups toasted chopped pecans

- In saucepan, cook cranberries in ¾ cup water on medium heat until skins break (about 15 minutes). Trim outside peel of 2 oranges and add to cranberries. Add juice from 1 orange and remaining ingredients, except pecans to cranberries and stir. Remove from heat and add pecans. Seal in small sterile jars with lids.

Slow-Cook Apple Butter

3 pounds baking apples, cored, peeled, finely chopped
4 cups sugar
4 teaspoons cinnamon
¼ teaspoon cloves

- Fill slow cooker heaping full with apples. (Lid may not fit at start, but apples shrink as they cook.) Drizzle sugar, cinnamon, cloves and ¼ teaspoon salt over apples. Cover and cook on HIGH for 1 hour.

- Lower heat, cook all day until thick and dark in color and stir occasionally. Pour into small glass jars and seal.

Homemade
Thousand Island Dressing

1 (1 pint) jar mayonnaise
1 (2 ounce) jar pimentos, drained
1 (12 ounce) jar sweet pickle relish
1 (12 ounce) bottle ketchup
3 eggs, hard-boiled, finely chopped

- In large bowl, combine all ingredients except eggs and mix well. Store in glass jar in refrigerator. Pour over favorite mixture of lettuce and vegetables and mix in eggs.

TIP: For added zip, you could add ½ teaspoon mustard or horseradish.

Ranch Dressing Mix

15 Saltines
2 cups dried parsley
½ cup dried minced onion
2 tablespoons dried dill weed
¼ cup onion salt
¼ cup garlic salt
¼ cup onion powder
¼ cup garlic powder

- Blend crackers in blender or food processor until they are powder. Stir in remaining ingredients and blend well. Pour into airtight container and store at room temperature for up to 1 year.

Salad Dressing:
1 tablespoon dry ranch-style salad dressing mix
1 cup mayonnaise
1 cup buttermilk

- Combine all ingredients. Makes 1 pint salad dressing.

Honey Mustard Sauce

⅓ cup honey
2 tablespoons dijon-style mustard
2 tablespoons brown sugar

- Combine all ingredients with 1 tablespoon water in saucepan and heat thoroughly.

263

Grilling with Horseradish

- Use prepared horseradish to coat all sides of meat to grill. With a paper towel, pat meat dry. The liquid and horseradish will keep the meat moist.

- Leave the horseradish on the grilled meat or scrape it off. Either way, horseradish adds a lot of flavor.

Horseradish Curls

- Scrub horseradish root and peel it like a potato.

- Shave or grate horseradish roots directly on meats or salads at the table. Place fine horseradish shavings in a dish of lemon juice before you serve dinner.

Horseradish Sauce

1½ cups buttermilk ranch dressing
¼ cup prepared horseradish

- Serve on your favorite cuts of beef.

In the United States, an estimated 24 million pounds of horseradish roots are ground and processed annually to produce approximately 6 million gallons of prepared horseradish.

Homemade Horseradish

1 horseradish root
White vinegar
Sugar

- Scrub horseradish root clean and peel it like a potato.
  (Horseradish may be grated by hand.) Dice root into small
  cubes and place a few cubes into glass blender.
  Add enough cold water to cover blades.

- Add crushed ice to blender and grind to coarse, almost
  smooth, consistency. Pour into measuring jar and repeat
  process with remaining horseradish. Add crushed ice to
  make grinding easier. Drain water from horseradish in
  measuring cup. For each 1 cup horseradish, mix as follows:
    1 cup ground horseradish
    2 - 3 tablespoons white vinegar
    1 teaspoon sugar, optional
    ½ teaspoon salt, optional

- For mild horseradish, add vinegar immediately. For really
  hot horseradish, wait 3 minutes to add vinegar.

- Place mixture in small glass jars with tight lids. Keep
  horseradish cold to keep it hot. It will keep for 4 to
  6 weeks in refrigerator and for 6 months in freezer.

TIP: Use a well-ventilated room to grind fresh horseradish!

Horseradish was first used around 1500 BC and
was appointed one of the "five bitter herbs" the
Jews were told to eat at Passover.

Horseradish Uses

Horseradish is a condiment. Depending on your taste, be as bold or mild as you wish. Add it fresh to foods for a sweet, hot taste. Add it to foods before you cook to give a mellow flavor that is not hot. Your options are varied.

Try it with:

Chili	Salads
Meatloaf	Salad dressings
Applesauce	Mayonnaise
Sauces	Butter
Gravies	Sour cream
Relishes	Ketchup
Dips	Potato salad
Cheese balls	Tartar sauce
Cheese spreads	Coleslaw

Illinois farmers from the Collinsville, IL area across the Mississippi River from St. Louis, grow about 60% of the world's supply of horseradish.

G

THE FARM FAMILY COOKBOOK INDEX

THE FARM FAMILY COOKBOOK INDEX

W

Z

COOKBOOKS PUBLISHED BY COOKBOOK RESOURCES, LLC

The Ultimate Cooking
with 4 Ingredients

Easy Cooking with 5 Ingredients

The Best of Cooking
with 3 Ingredients

Gourmet Cooking with 5 Ingredients

Healthy Cooking with 4 Ingredients

Diabetic Cooking with 4 Ingredients

4-Ingredient Recipes for
30-Minute Meals

Essential 3-4-5 Ingredient Recipes

The Best 1001 Short, Easy Recipes

Easy Slow-Cooker Cookbook

Easy 1-Dish Meals

Easy Potluck Recipes

Essential Slow-Cooker Cooking

Quick Fixes with Cake Mixes

Casseroles to the Rescue

Easy Casseroles

I Ain't On No Diet Cookbook

Kitchen Keepsakes/
More Kitchen Keepsakes

Old-Fashioned Cookies

Grandmother's Cookies

Mother's Recipes

Recipe Keeper

Cookie Dough Secrets

Gifts for the Cookie Jar

All New Gifts for the Cookie Jar

Gifts in a Pickle Jar

Muffins In A Jar

Brownies In A Jar

Cookie Jar Magic

Easy Desserts

Bake Sale Bestsellers

Quilters' Cooking Companion

Miss Sadie's Southern Cooking

Southern Family Favorites

Classic Tex-Mex and Texas Cooking

Classic Southwest Cooking

The Great Canadian Cookbook

The Best of Lone Star
Legacy Cookbook

Cookbook 25 Years

Pass the Plate

Texas Longhorn Cookbook

Trophy Hunters' Wild Game
Cookbook

Mealtimes and Memories

Holiday Recipes

Little Taste of Texas

Little Taste of Texas II

Southwest Sizzler

Southwest Olé

Class Treats

Leaving Home

Italian Family Cookbook

Sunday Nigh Suppers

365 Easy Meals

365 Easy Chicken

365 Soups and Stews

To Order: **The Farm Family Cookbook**

Please send _____ paperback copies @ $16.95 (U.S.) each $ _____

Texas residents add sales tax @ $1.36 each $ _____

Plus postage/handling @ $6.00 (1st copy) $ _____

$1.00 (each additional copy) $ _____

Check or Credit Card (Canada-credit card only) Total $ _____

Charge to: ❏ MasterCard   or   ❏ VISA

Account # _____

Expiration Date _____

Signature_____

Name _____

Address_____

City_____State_____Zip_____

Telephone (day_____(Evening)_____

Mail or Call:
Cookbook Resources
541 Doubletree Dr.
Highland Village, Texas 75077
Toll Free (866) 229-2665
(972) 317-6404 Fax

To Order: **The Farm Family Cookbook**

Please send _____ paperback copies @ $16.95 (U.S.) each $ _____

Texas residents add sales tax @ $1.36 each $ _____

Plus postage/handling @ $6.00 (1st copy) $ _____

$1.00 (each additional copy) $ _____

Check or Credit Card (Canada-credit card only) Total $ _____

Charge to: ❏ MasterCard   or   ❏ VISA

Account # _____

Expiration Date _____

Signature_____

Name _____

Address_____

City_____State_____Zip_____

Telephone (day_____(Evening)_____

Mail or Call:
Cookbook Resources
541 Doubletree Dr.
Highland Village, Texas 75077
Toll Free (866) 229-2665
(972) 317-6404 Fax